# WARRIOR QUEENS

## TRUE STORIES OF SIX ANCIENT REBELS WHO SLAYED HISTORY

**VICKY ALVEAR SHECTER**    illustrated by **BILL MAYER**

BOYDS MILLS PRESS
AN IMPRINT OF BOYDS MILLS AND KANE
*New York*

Boyds Mills Press
An Imprint of Boyds Mills & Kane
boydsmillspress.com
Printed in the United States of America

ISBN: 978-1-62979-679-6 • ebook ISBN: 978-1-68437-899-9
Book data is on file with the Library of Congress.

First edition
10 9 8 7 6 5 4 3 2 1

Design by Barbara Grzeslo
The type is set in Sabon.
The illustrations are done in a combination of traditional and digital media. The art was first drawn in pen and ink and then scanned. Additional elements such as textures, spatters, and patterns were added digitally.

*For all the warrior queens in my life.*

# ACKNOWLEDGMENTS

A huge thank you to the professors, experts, archaeologists, and curators who read through these pages for accuracy. Any mistakes or misrepresentations of historical records are mine and mine alone. Many, many thanks to Egyptologist Clare Fitzgerald, Associate Director for Exhibitions and Gallery Curator at the Institute for the Study of the Ancient World at New York University; Adrienne Mayor, author and Classics Professor at Stanford University; Caroline Rocheleau, Curator of Egyptian/Nubian art at the North Carolina Museum of Art; Christoph Giebel, Professor of International Studies and History at the University of Washington; Jessica Clark, Classics Professor at Florida State University; and Judith Weingarten, archaeologist and professor at the British School at Athens/Knossos. Also thank you to my sensitivity readers, Robyn Lucas and Tam Hoang, for jumping in and offering insight.

And, of course, a huge Amazonian queen high five to Larry Rosler, who encouraged me to submit the book, and to editors Mary L. Colgan and Andrea Cascardi, as well as everyone at Boyds Mills Press who helped make this book a reality!

# INTRODUCTION
## Bloodthirsty Warriors in Crowns

Some ancient queens were fabulous. Others were fierce. The best were both—brilliant leaders who expertly ruled their kingdoms while furiously fighting anyone who dared threaten them or their people.

The ancient world was particularly brutal to women. Men made laws and rules to keep women out of power, uneducated, and often hidden from the public world. Yet these six queens came roaring out of their palaces like lionesses protecting their cubs, ready to eviscerate challengers and enemies alike.

And eviscerate them they did! Unfortunately, we don't have records of *how* these women fought because often it was the queens' enemies who recorded their stories. You know, the very men angriest about being bested by women. So the victors often downplayed the women's talents, abilities, and victories. It was almost as if male recordkeepers found losing to women somehow . . . *embarrassing*.

Luckily, modern scholars are able to fill in some of the holes with archaeological evidence. The result is a look into the lives of women who prized razor-sharp swords and armor-piercing arrows just as much as jewel-encrusted crowns of gold.

Most of the ancient warrior queens in these stories didn't

go looking for trouble. It came to them, usually at the hands of invaders who wanted to steal their land and power. Every single one of these queens pushed back hard.

*Not on my watch,* they cried.

All of them were prepared to die fighting for their queendoms. Some of them did, choosing death on the battlefield rather than submitting to their enemies. They fought in chariots, on ships, and even on elephants, wielding weapons that cut right to the heart (and often right *into* the heart) of the matter.

These fearless queens were more than ready to throw down against the biggest, meanest, baddest guys who dared challenge them. They were powerful women who laughed in the face of their enemies, women who had one message for anyone who claimed they shouldn't or couldn't stand up to invaders: *Watch me slay.*

# TIMELINE:

*Dates indicate when these queens either came to power or took up arms against enemies.*

## 1492 BCE (before the Common Era):
### HATSHEPSUT of Egypt

## 480 BCE:
### ARTEMISIA I of Halicarnassus

## 27 BCE:
### AMANIRENAS of Nubia

## 39–40 CE (Common Era):
### THE TRUNG SISTERS of Vietnam

## 60 CE:
### BOUDICCA of Britain

## 269 CE:
### ZENOBIA of Palmyra (Syria)

## CHAPTER ONE

# HATSHEPSUT

## THE WOMAN WHO RULED AS A MAN

Hatshepsut was the most powerful female pharaoh to ever rule in Egypt. Yet within three generations after her death, the average Egyptian had likely never heard of her. In fact, most ancient Egyptians didn't even know she'd *existed*.

Which is a bit like Americans never having heard of Susan B. Anthony. Or Britons unfamiliar with Elizabeth I. Or . . . well, the Justice League not knowing about Wonder Woman.

The problem was that nearly every record of Hatshepsut's rule nearly 3,500 years ago had been viciously destroyed.

Hatshepsut's successor didn't want people to remember just how successfully she ruled as pharaoh or how aggressively she masterminded a foreign invasion. He tried to keep her story—along with her mummy—under wraps. Thankfully, modern

Egyptologists have begun digging up the truth and unraveling the facts of her amazing run as the most powerful woman of her era.

## What We Do Know

Hatshepsut ruled in what Egyptologists call the Eighteenth Dynasty, which refers to the era of her family's power during the fifteenth century before the Common Era (BCE). Hatshepsut's father was the great general Thutmose I.

Daddy Thut (no, not King Tut—he came about 150 years *after* Hatshepsut) was a tough military guy. He also had a flair for drama. After a victory in Africa, he sailed home with the naked body of the defeated king dangling from the prow of his ship.[1] King Thut, it seemed, liked to keep his enemies in line—or hanging from one anyway. But he had terrible luck with a different kind of line: the line of succession.

King Thut's royal children all died young, except for one daughter—Hatshepsut. To keep the power in the family, he had her marry her younger half-brother (Thut's son by a minor wife), Thutmose II.

Yes, you read that right—she had to marry her *brother*. But that was nothing new in ancient Egypt. Royal brother-sister marriages were typical because they kept the power within the family. And to the Egyptians, a stable family of intermarried rulers was preferable to constant wars for control of the throne.

The practice was so accepted for royalty, in fact, that the Egyptians even had brother-sister gods who intermarried, such as Isis and Osiris and Set and Nephthys.

That's not to say that Hatshepsut was happy with the arrangement. We'll never know what she really thought because we don't have any of her letters or diaries. But based on her behavior, we can guess that she wouldn't have hesitated to do whatever was necessary to keep her beloved Egypt strong and stable.

Like the lion-bodied sphinx overlooking the pyramids, protecting Egypt was her *mane* concern.

## The Tween Queen

Hatshepsut was twelve or thirteen when she married her little brother.[2] She had a child soon after—a daughter named Neferure. In other words, Hatshepsut became a queen, wife, and mother before most modern kids get out of middle school.

To be fair, in the ancient world, a girl was considered a woman the moment she was physically able to get pregnant. And with high mortality rates—with people only living on average to about thirty-five years—you could say being in your mid-teens was like being middle-aged.

Unfortunately, Hatshepsut's brother-husband became a low life-expectancy statistic.[3] He died about three years after taking the throne, but not before having a son with a different, minor wife.

Hatshepsut was left a widow at about sixteen. And because she'd had a girl child, she was about to be left out in the cold too. In ancient Egypt, a baby boy outranked even the most royal queen.

## "I Know . . . Put the Baby in Charge!"

According to ancient rules and practices, only a boy could rule Egypt. The pharaoh's son, however, was still quite young when his father's body was shipped off to the local mummifier. Since babies make terrible rulers (think of the tantrums!), other power-hungry people likely tried to push their way into power. There may have even been talk of assassinations and military takeovers.

But by sheer force of will, our plucky queen put a stop to all that. She came up with a plan that made everyone happy: she would rule as a substitute—or as regent—until the baby, Thutmose III, was old enough to take the throne.

In other words, she would hold his place in line.[4]

This made sense because she had the most royal blood of anyone in the palace. Since the Egyptians believed royals were partly divine, Hatshepsut used this to her advantage. But the queen didn't rest on the royalty of her family's line alone—she impressed everyone with her smarts and gumption too.

She stabilized the government and calmed everyone's fears of enemy invasions by strengthening Egypt's borders. She appeased the powerful priests of Amun. And she kept the economy strong

16

by building roadways, sanctuaries, and impressive monuments.

While Hollywood movies imply that slaves built Egypt's great monuments, the truth is that free laborers and farmers did most of the work for their pharaohs in exchange for food and oil and, often, housing during the farming off-season. Not every ruler was willing to finance projects that benefited the average person. Hatshepsut, however, invested heavily in projects to spread the wealth. She also encouraged artistic innovation. Her mortuary at Deir el-Bahri is often cited as one of the most beautiful temples in all of Egypt.

But her commitment to the people and economy of Egypt was just the beginning. The young queen also proved her awesomeness with the sword when she invaded a foreign power.

Without a doubt, Hatshepsut knew how to keep her enemies on edge.

## Like Father, Like Daughter

Remember how her father, Thutmose I, sailed home with the naked body of a defeated king dangling from the prow of his ship? Hatshepsut sought to prove herself as Egypt's true leader by stringing up a line of victories of her own too.[5]

So she invaded regions south of Egypt, likely in today's Sudan, which the Egyptians called Nubia. We don't have details of the battle, but one of the queen's officials, named Ty, wrote that he "followed" her into battle and that she *destroyed* the land of Nubia.[6] Hatshepsut's treasurer, a guy named Djehuty, wrote on his tomb that he "counted up ivory, ebony, and the many fruits of" the Nubian invasion, implying that he'd accompanied her.[7]

Some scholars also believe that she either led forces into the regions that are called Syria and Israel today or at least stood up to invaders harassing her borders. She bragged about protecting Egypt's territories from these invaders by carving on her temple that those "eastern frontier[s] . . . across the sand of Asia are in my grip."[8]

When it came to owning her power by the sword, Hatshepsut did not hesitate to cut deep.

## Chariot Queen on a Roll

While we don't have details about Hatshepsut in battle, we can assume—based on what we know about Egyptian warfare of the period—that she fought on wheels.[9] Egyptian chariots usually carried two warriors: one to manage the horses, the other to smite the enemy with heavy compound bows. And if that didn't work, foot soldiers sliced and diced the leftovers with curved swords called *khopesh*.

Hatshepsut's military victories were exceeded only by her smart business and trade deals, which brought even more wealth into the kingdom. Thanks to her, Egypt was awash in gold, ebony, ivory, incense, wild animals, and other money-making goods. The economy soared.

People got rich.

And Hatshepsut had shown everyone that she could arm

up and kick butt in war, just like her father and all the other great pharaohs before her. Despite ruling for nearly a decade, one thing was still missing: a formal title.

Hatshepsut *ruled* liked a pharaoh. She went on military and trade expeditions like a pharaoh. She even built impressive monuments like a pharaoh. But as a woman, she wasn't allowed to *be* pharaoh.

Hatshepsut wasn't about to let old traditions stop her. So she came up with a solution that gave her instant legitimacy.

## Who's Your Daddy?

Claiming pharaoh-hood was leveling up to a whole new category of power and not everyone was ready for it. So the queen began telling a new story—that the creator god Amun was her actual father. This put a divine stamp of approval on her naming herself pharaoh. She also claimed that an oracle had foretold her kingship, describing Amun's selection of her. And who could argue with the gods?

Hatshepsut the queen regent had officially become Hatshepsut the pharaoh, the divinely approved ruler of the Two Lands.

At the same time, Hatshepsut gave her stepson (Thutmose III) all the best training available, including learning the art of war from Egypt's top generals. In other words, she took full power—including the title of pharaoh—*without* undermining the kid who would one day take her place.

That is some kind of finesse.

How did she do it? Apparently very, very carefully.

First and foremost, she got the support of the most powerful and important officials—including the priests of Amun—in the kingdom. And also of all of her military generals. No one quite knows how she accomplished this, but it likely involved sharing a great deal of the wealth that she'd brought in from the middle of Africa. But her success also implies that she had a talent for winning people over and inspiring confidence.

People call that *charisma*, and she must have had plenty to spare because no queen before her had ever dared to take on as much power with so little resistance. It's kind of like the water girl taking over as lead striker at the Women's World Cup soccer finals and winning the championship with ease.

## Say No to the Dress

Like a smartphone user discovering hidden filters, Hatshepsut knew that small adjustments to her image had a big impact on the way people perceived her, so she began slowly editing how she was represented in art. In the early years, she was shown as a woman in a long dress, wearing a king's crown.[10] Then, for a little while, she kept the dress but had her shoulders broadened and was shown striding forth like a man.

Slowly her image transformed until she ended up losing the dress and wearing the kilt—and sometimes the beard—of a king. She was shown as a muscular young man, often receiving blessings from the gods. The message was that the gods approved of her rule, and that she was strong enough to rule Egypt, protect her borders, build impressive structures, and perform all of the kingly rituals required to maintain *maat* (mah-*at*).[11]

*Maat* was the word the Egyptians used to describe a force for order in the world, a balance that kept everybody safe. But as long as Hatshepsut was only a regent, the country technically had no ruling pharaoh. No pharaoh, some worried, meant no maat. And no maat meant bad things were going to happen.

So, Hatshepsut did what she needed to do to reassure everyone. By taking the throne as pharaoh, she maintained maat. She kept the world ordered and peaceful. Things were under control. Everything was going to be okay.

And really, for more than twenty years, it was.

## Enter the Young King

By all accounts, Hatshepsut's rule rocked. She squashed her enemies, expanded the kingdom, made the country prosper and the arts flourish, and had some of the greatest architecture of all time built in her name. Even better, the pharaoh-queen had prepared her stepson for kingship so well that the transfer of power after she died was easy and seamless.

Thutmose III ruled after her for more than thirty years. Egypt continued to thrive, and he expanded its borders even more with further campaigns against Nubia and Syria. You'd think he would've been grateful. But instead, he hip checked Hatshepsut into the pit of oblivion. Why?

## The Evil Stepmother Theory

Archaeologists found proof of Hatshepsut's reign in the early twentieth century when they discovered a pit filled with destroyed statues of the kingly queen. Her statues were toppled, her name had been hacked away, and every evidence of her rule was either disguised or tossed.

Only a pharaoh could've made that happen, so they figured Thutmose III must have really, *really* hated Hatshepsut. Debates on why he turned on her grew to a fever pitch around the same time that a guy named Disney released a little movie called *Snow White* in 1938.

Suddenly, a theory that sounded very much like a Disney movie took hold. And it went something like this: *Hatshepsut was a "wicked stepmother" who stole the kingdom right from under poor, innocent Thutmose III's nose. But the good king eventually grew up and took his revenge, only her punishment was erasure instead of being chased off a mountain by avenging dwarfs.*[12]

But honestly, if she were all that evil, wouldn't she have simply killed Thutmose III when he was a little kid? But she didn't. Instead, she made sure he got the best education, including military training.

And thanks to that military training, King Thut III became known as one of the greatest pharaohs of all time, expanding Egyptian territory through conquests deep into Africa, Syria, and today's Israel.

By all accounts, Hatshepsut did a great job of raising him as her successor. Thutmose III may have even been grateful to his stepmom for keeping things stable in Egypt until he could take over.[13]

But if he were grateful, he sure had a funny way of showing it! The mystery deepened.

## Twenty-Year Time-Out

Things got a little clearer when modern archaeologists learned that King Thut III didn't start defacing and erasing Hatshepsut's history until the end of his reign, more than twenty years *after* her death, so it didn't look like a crime of passion. After all, why wait decades if you're mad about something *now*?

Today, most experts believe he waited to tamper with her image until he was close to death to ensure that his son would rule after him. Erasing Hatshepsut made it look like he took the throne directly from his father. This way, he could pass the throne to his own son without any problems—which he did.

Thutmose III may have had other motivations as well, including the fact that Hatshepsut's success made Egyptians nervous. He may have wanted to prevent the possibility that another powerful woman might ever take over and mess with the long line of Egyptian male kings.

And his male ego may also have been a bit bruised. Thutmose III, a "stickler for tradition," simply may not have liked the idea of being the guy who followed the famous female pharaoh.[14] If that's true, then it probably wasn't even personal. He just wanted to control his image—and that meant erasing the fact that a woman ruled before him.

Whatever the reason, Thutmose III failed. Many people today have at least heard of Hatshepsut. But few know about Thutmose III!

He may have successfully erased her for thousands of years, but in the end, the truth won out. And Hatshepsut's legacy lives on.

◇ ◇ ◇

### Was Hatshepsut a Queen or a Pharaoh?

Both, actually. When Hatshepsut was married to Thutmose II, she was called the God's Wife, consort to the ruler of the Two Lands of Egypt, which made her queen. But as she took more and more control of the kingdom, she ascended to pharaoh, which is kind of like going from being a benchwarmer on the junior varsity team to most valuable player in the major leagues.

In other words, it was a huge upgrade—Hatshepsut went from being married to a god to *being* a god. Pharaohs were considered divine, or part god, and ruled over everything—politics, religion, the military, even all the land.

Farmers paid rent and/or taxes for working the pharaoh's fields and farms. Those who were poor toiled at the bottom of society, while the pharaoh was at the top of the pyramid (in every way possible).

Besides their main job of maintaining maat, pharaohs also had full religious authority, as well as total political and military control, which meant Hatshepsut had the unique ability to pray, slay, and conquer the day—all at once.

Or at least until Thutmose III came along and pretended she never existed.

### "If I Don't See You, You Don't Exist . . ."

Egyptians believed images had power. Real power. As in, if you destroyed someone's image, you seriously hurt their chances for life in the afterworld. It would be like a second death. And once was enough, thank you very much.

But even more important than an image was the *body* of the dead. It was needed to house the *ka*, or individual spirit, of the recently deceased. No body, no afterlife, which was why mummification was so important to the Egyptians.

It's interesting that despite smashing Hatshepsut's statues and carving over her images, Thutmose III didn't touch her mummy. After all, if he had really wanted to put the hurt on her, he would've destroyed her remains. But then again, it's just as possible that he may have tried to get rid of the mummy. Hatshepsut's body was found stashed in someone else's coffin. Perhaps her priests and devotees hid it to keep her stepson from destroying it. We'll never know.

Thutmose III also left alone the images that showed Hatshepsut as queen rather than pharaoh.[15] A woman's "place" as queen was acceptable, he seemed to say, but he drew the line at images of the queen as pharaoh.

For all his fame as a powerful pharaoh, when it came to how he treated Hatshepsut's memory, Thutmose III was the king of *de-Nile*.

25

## I Want My Mummy:
## The Queen Is Finally Uncovered!

Egyptian archaeologists should've gotten an award for their *dead*-ication in finally unwrapping the mystery of Hatshepsut's mummy.

Using DNA, CT scans, and a tooth found in a box bearing Hatshepsut's name, they finally identified the mummy that went with her tooth. That and several other tests confirmed in 2007 that a mummy previously thought to be Hatshepsut's nursemaid was actually the great queen herself. [16]

Hatshepsut's body had been hidden in plain sight, jumbled amongst a group of mummified servants. Someone must have worried that a royal burial would have drawn too much attention—or anger—and stashed her in a safe place.

Her preserved body gave us a lot of information. She stood about 5'2" and was obese. How they do know? The tummy of the mummy was quite a bit larger than most others'. Plus, instead of a cut in the abdomen to pull out her organs, the mummy makers had to go in through the hips. Tests also showed the queen suffered from cancer and a bone disease called osteoporosis.

Hatshepsut's mummy was originally dug up at the turn of the century. But because it had no identifying clues, archaeologists had shoved it aside for more showy discoveries. It was only in the last several years that archaeologists began using the latest technology to unwrap the truth.

### Egyptian Gods and Their Pyramid Schemes

The ancient Egyptians believed in thousands of gods. Most represented aspects of nature they depended on, such as the sun, air, the Nile River, and so on.

Pyramids were initially tombs for powerful pharaohs, who were considered partly divine. To evoke the sense of power and grandeur of the gods, the tops of pyramids were gilded so they shone in the sun, while the rest of the structure was sheathed in shining limestone, creating a breathtaking reminder of their leader's connection to the sun and their most powerful creator-god, Amun.

Originally, only pharaohs were mummified. Their bodies were preserved so that their spirits had a "house" to live in while they helped the gods fight the unseen forces of chaos and evil. Over time, wealthy nobles wanted a piece of eternal life too, and they began to pay powerful priests to be embalmed. Only instead of fighting alongside the gods to protect the people, ordinary Egyptians got to live in a beautiful place for eternity. Eventually, the practice grew in popularity so that a great many ancient Egyptians— particularly those who had the means to pay for it—could live happily ever after. Literally.

But only if they lived good, ordered, kind lives. If they were bad or evil, they were not allowed in. *Tut-tut!*

❖

## CHAPTER NOTES

[1]— Most of Egypt's gold came from Nubia (today's northern Sudan). Egypt and Nubia had a long history of trading goods, but every once in a while, they battled each other like sisters reaching for the last cookie in the cookie jar. Thutmose I displayed the body of a Kushite king "hanging upside from the prow of the royal boat" as a warning to potential enemies.

27

[2] — She was left as the "most mature and educated surviving child" of the family. Imagine the pressure!

[3] — "Life expectancy in ancient Egypt was in the early thirties for men, perhaps fifty for an elite . . ." So really, for some, living to their teens was like being middle-aged!

[4] — Holding his place in line was the original idea, but over time, she demanded more and more control. "She simply overpowered him."

Hatshepsut's funerary temple at Deir El-Bahri is considered one of the most impressive monuments of its kind.

[5]— Old-school thinkers just assumed a female pharaoh wasn't warlike, but one modern scholar says, "there is evidence that Hatshepsut may have led a campaign into Nubia."

[6]— According to historian W. V. Davies, Chancellor Ty was the official was who bragged that he saw Hatshepsut "ravaging" Nubia.

[7]— Djehuty seemed to want *everyone* to know that Hatshepsut was his queen and that she dominated Nubia.

[8]— Hatshepsut bragged about holding the line on her borders against invaders on obelisks at her temple at Deir El-Bahri.

[9]— We have lots of paintings of pharaohs fighting in chariots. We also have a war supply list from Hatshepsut's successor that includes horses and chariots.

[10]—In the beginning, she "continued to use the insignia and titular of a king's principal wife."

[11]—The pharaoh stood between the divine and human worlds. He was the bridge—the one who kept "the universe functioning" for the people—the maintainer of order, that is, maat.

[12]—Archaeologists in the 1920s and 30s called Hatshepsut "the vilest type of usurper" and claimed that Thutmose III had developed a "loathing for Hatshepsut . . . which practically beggars description." Modern scholars think this view reflected the sexism of the era.

[13]—Hatshepsut included carved representations of Thutmose III in her monuments throughout Egypt and Nubia, as well as her temple. Why would she do that unless she

was paving the way for him to take over? She was bolstering—not diminishing—his claim to rule after her. [14]—One Hatshepsut expert suggests that "wounded male pride" may have played a part in Thutmose's plan to erase Hatshepsut's history. That's a nice way of saying fragile male egos were involved.

Hatshepsut understood the power of imagery. She depicted herself as male and a lion-bodied sphinx, which represented strength and protection.

[15]—Her enemies seemed to like it when she was clearly represented as a woman. A. M. Roth writes, "Some quite feminine depictions of the queen were left intact."

[16]—Egyptologist Zahi Hawass, who led the search for Hatshepsut's mummy, says the tests proved that the mummy in question was indeed "the mummy of Queen Hatshepsut." Other scholars take a more cautious approach and agree that the evidence shows that the body is "probably" Hatshepsut's. The mummy now resides in the Royal Mummies Room of the Egyptian Museum in Cairo.

## CHAPTER TWO

# ARTEMISIA 1

## AMAZON OF THE SEAS

At a time when most ordinary women had no power at all, one ancient queen commanded a fleet, kicked butt at sea, and proved herself a seriously crafty leader.

Her name was Artemisia I. And she played a fascinating role in the world-changing war between the ancient Greeks and Persians.

Artemisia's *admiral*-able leadership left her allies impressed and her enemies . . . well, under the sea. So how did a Greek woman end up as a warrior of the waves?

It all began when, as a princess of a Greek city-state in Anatolia (today's Turkey, which at the time was controlled by the Persian kingdom), Artemisia married the king of a neighboring city-state called Caria. We know nothing of her husband except that when he died, he left her in charge. And take charge she did!

Soon Queen Artemisia wasn't content to rule just her kingdom—she went on a military campaign for more land and resources. Using brains rather than brawn, she successfully ambushed a rich coastal city without shedding a single drop of blood.

And all it took was a little planning.

## "Best Party Ever!"

Artemisia discovered that there was a sacred grove devoted to the Mother Goddess just outside Latmus, the city she wanted to take, so she directed her soldiers to hide around the perimeter while she led a huge procession of worshippers toward the grove.

Throwing flowers, making music, singing, twirling, and stomping to the beat, Artemisia and her procession of colorfully dressed women and priests made a spectacle of themselves as they paraded toward the sacred wood. Not wanting to miss the celebration, the city's watchmen and citizens rushed outside to join the fun.

And while they were away, the queen's soldiers quietly took the city. Artemisia's ploy took the idea of a surprise party to a whole new level.

One ancient historian described her victory as winning by "flutes and cymbals" rather than by "a force of arms."[1]

But that was only the beginning. It was her smarts at sea that anchored her reputation as one of history's most brilliant naval commanders.

## The Battle of the Superpowers

For decades, two major powers fought for supremacy—the Greeks and the Persians. Greece consisted of multiple city-states on the Greek peninsula. They were a quarrelsome bunch that often fought neighbors from other Greek city-states.

The Persians, on the other hand, ruled a vast area in the Middle East in the region where the countries of Iran, Iraq, Turkey, Syria, Egypt, Libya, and others are located today.[2] Persia was one of the first multicultural kingdoms in the world, with people of very different cultures speaking multiple languages and all agreeing to call the Persian king their supreme leader.[3]

This is where Artemisia comes in because even though she was Greek and spoke Greek, she fought *for* the Persians. Over the centuries, Greeks had begun settling in areas that would later fall under Persian rule, mostly in today's Turkey. But eventually the Persian king decided that if Greek city-states were going to be on his land, then *all* of Greece needed to be under his rule too.

Artemisia was fine with this. After all, her family and kingdom had spent generations on Persian soil. Other Greek city-states on Persian land were not so accommodating. *Nope,* they said. *We're staying Greek, thank you very much.* This often led to local wars and skirmishes.

Persian kings grew tired of those pesky Greek independents. After a while, they figured that it would make more sense to conquer the whole region. Then the Greek city-states on Persian land would have no backup from the Greek mainland. And Persia's kingdom and power base would grow even stronger.

Persia's first attempt at invading Greece didn't go very well. Persia captured a couple of city-states, but not Athens, which was turning into the heart of defiance against it.

Nearly a decade after the first invasion, King Xerxes I (*zurk-sees*) decided to attack again. He sent Greece a demand: *I won't attack you if you claim me as your over-king. To seal our bargain, you must send me earth and water—all that sustains you—as proof that I now own you.*[4]

Terrified, some Greek city-states complied, sending over leather bags of dirt as proof of their surrender.

Meanwhile, Athens and Sparta, among others, refused to soil themselves in such a way.

It was war. And Artemisia prepared to fight alongside the Persian king.

## By Land and Sea

With Artemisia leading as one of its generals, Persia came at Greece with massive land and sea forces. The Greeks responded by divvying up the fighting: Sparta would fight on land, while Athens, with its superior navy, would fight at sea against Artemisia and the other naval commanders.

While Artemisia and her fleet prepared to engage on the waves, 300 Spartans, along with 7,000 allies from other Greek city-states, tried to block the Persians from marching into Greece through a narrow land pass called Thermopylae.[5] Like Gandalf from the *Lord of the Rings*, the Greeks might as well have shouted, "You shall not pass!"

The Persians' response? *OMG, you guys are so cute!*

After all, scholars estimate they had more than 100,000 warriors to the Greeks' 7,000.[6]

Amazingly, the Greeks held off the Persians for days. Eventually, Xerxes learned of an alternate path and snuck around the Greeks. When the Spartan King Leonidas learned about their maneuver, he urged most of the Greeks at Thermopylae to leave before they could be encircled. He and his Spartans would hold the Persians back to give the other Greek armies the chance to make it out and fight another day.

The 300 Spartan warriors died that day, desperately defending the pass.[7]

The Persians got through anyway. They marched all the way to Athens, the city-state that had been developing a political system called democracy, where every citizen had a vote.

Too bad for Athens, the Persians elected to shut them down.

The city was sacked and burned to the ground.

The Persian victory on land probably gave Artemisia and her fellow admirals the sense that a naval victory was going to be a walk on the beach.

They were in for a whale of a surprise.

## Artemisia Steps Up

At first, Artemisia and the rest of the Persian navy had Greek boats on the run.[8]

The queen brought with her a fleet of five triremes and up to 1,000 sailors and fighters. How she learned to fight and command a navy no one knows, but Xerxes certainly had faith in her. After all, he invited her to his inner circle of war advisors.

Persian culture respected women as leaders, queens, generals, and priests. Despite Artemisia's Greek heritage—where women had no power—the queen clearly took advantage of the opportunities her adopted nation encouraged.

But to the Greeks, a woman military leader was almost unimaginable. Greek women could not own property or vote and had few legal rights. They were considered the property of men. They had to hide in the house and were not allowed to go to school. Most weren't even allowed to eat at the same table as men. Their main purpose, the ancients believed, was to care for children and weave clothing. The Greeks' general disrespect toward women ran so deep, the worst insult you could give a man was to say that he acted "like a woman."

Unsurprisingly, Artemisia became a source of anxious fascination. They could not believe they were fighting against a woman, let alone a woman who dressed like a Persian man—wearing pants and carrying a sword and dagger! They were outraged.[9] And insulted.

But by the time Artemisia was done, the Greeks would've been proud to fight like her.

## Hungry for the Battle of Salamis

Despite its name, the Battle of Salamis did not involve cold cuts. Salamis was a Greek city on an island near the Greek mainland. The Athenian navy had retreated to the straits of Salamis to regroup as the Persians advanced by sea.

When Athenian sailors learned that their city had been sacked, they lost hope. Most Greeks were ready to give up, but one smart commander had several tricks up his tunic.

A Greek officer sent word to the Persians that he and his Athenian navy were turning traitor. Xerxes knew that his superior numbers—he had more than 1,300 warships—gave the Persians a huge advantage.[10] Combined with word that a key Greek leader was secretly planning to defect to his side, he figured that wiping out the Greek navy was a sure thing.

He was wrong.

But only one plucky queen had the backbone to tell him the truth.

## "You Are Making a Serious Mistake, Your Eminence."

Xerxes called a council of all his most trusted naval commanders—including Artemisia—to determine his strategy. They all said, "Continue the fight at sea." Sure, they admitted, the

Greeks were better sailors, but their own significantly larger numbers made them unbeatable.

Only Artemisia was strong enough to stand up and speak her mind.

According to Herodotus, Artemisia said: "Spare your ships, and do not risk a battle; for these people are as much superior to your people in seamanship, as men to women." Yes, she threw other women under the chariot wheels, but she likely did so to surprise the king with how strongly she believed that they were outmatched. After all, the Greeks were famous for being excellent sailors. Persia, on the other hand, was dominant on land.

The queen continued: "What so great need is there for you to incur hazard at sea? Are you not master of Athens, for which you did undertake your expedition? Is not Hellas [the Greeks] subject to you? Not a soul now resists your advance."[11]

In other words, you accomplished your main goal. Stop *trawling* for more trouble. It's time to sail on.

Silence must have filled the great king's tent, parked as they were on the island overlooking the straits of Salamis. No one had ever dared speak to the Persian king of kings so bluntly. But Artemisia didn't stop there. She went on to advise the king on land strategy too.

"Surround the land with your fleet," she suggested. "The Greeks are almost out of food. We just need to wait them out. They will fall apart, and then you can take Athens without any major losses of your navy. Your land forces will have no problem."

Her friends and enemies alike in the chamber had told the king to fight at sea. Her advice was so contrary, the other men must have all grabbed their throats in a reflex of sympathetic protection. Surely, they figured, Xerxes would have her head for speaking so bluntly to him.

Instead, the king was impressed.

He had always liked Artemisia, but now he praised her above others for her analysis and bravery in speaking out.

By expressing her opinion, she had shown fearlessness, tact, and incisive wisdom.

So the king did exactly what you'd expect from a man of his era: he ignored her advice anyway and pretended she'd never spoken.

## "Seriously? Did You Even Hear Me?"

Artemisia must have stared openmouthed as the king announced that they would do the opposite of what she recommended: they would engage the seafaring experts by sea.

Why? Despite Artemisia's cautions, Xerxes must have figured more was better. After all, he had the far larger fleet and bigger, heavier ships. Using thick, metal-tipped prows, he planned on crushing all of the Greeks' boats into floating masses of splintered wood.

But while the Persians were fighting for dominance, the Greeks were fighting for something more—everything they knew and loved. In other words, they were fighting with heart.

It made a difference.

Meanwhile, Xerxes was so sure of victory he marched up to the top of a cliff overlooking the sea to watch the combat. It didn't take long, though, to realize that his navy was in a boatload of trouble.

## Chasing the Queen

Try to imagine an ancient sea battle: Bronze-beaked ships rammed into each other with great splintering crashes. If the shattered hulls didn't sink a ship right away, soldiers swarmed onto each other's boats and fought by hand—with swords and knives and bows and arrows.

Blood slicked the decks as warriors tried to cut each other to pieces. Between the sounds of breaking ships, the clanging of weapons, and the screams of the dying, it must have been a nightmare of gore, agony, and chaos.

Amidst the carnage, it was probably hard to tell who was fighting on whose side.

Through it all, Artemisia's fleet held its own until one Athenian warship zeroed in on her ship, determined to take it out.

The enemy bore down on her vessel. Her only chance of survival was to escape, but a fellow Persian's ship had her blocked.

Artemisia had a choice: ram and sink her ally's ship to

get away, or stop and be captured by the Greeks. She chose to crash her way out, no matter the cost.

That's right. She deliberately sank her own buddy's ship!

Her attack on a fellow Persian confused the advancing Greeks. The captain figured either Artemisia's boat was Greek—an ally—or that it was a Persian deserter now on his side. So he gave orders to let her ship go and turned away to engage a different enemy ship.

The queen had outmaneuvered her enemy to survive. And, as the Persian navy endured huge losses, this was no small thing.

It's likely that Artemisia performed many other impressive feats that kept her navy largely intact, but since it was her enemies—the Greeks—who told her story, those feats are lost to us.

Nevertheless, she proved to the world that, as a naval commander, she was ready to overcome any *oar-deal*.

## "Impressive. Most Impressive."

Artemisia's daring maneuvers so impressed the Persian king, he remarked, "Today my men have fought like women, my women like men."[12] Later, a Greek historian would claim no other commander was worth mentioning by name.[13]

Artemisia's ingenuity was in sharp contrast to the seafaring abilities of both her allies *and* enemies. But it wasn't enough to save Xerxes's forces. Despite being outnumbered, the Greeks trounced the Persian fleet. The strait turned dark with blood and was clogged with splintered boats and floating body parts—most of them Persian. The carnage took the wind out of Xerxes's sails. He called for a retreat. And not just at sea.

When he learned his land forces—despite burning Athens to the ground—were also getting seriously harassed, he called the whole thing off. The invasion was over. It was time to go home.

## The Queen as Body Collector

After the call to retreat, the Greeks were determined to destroy every Persian ship that had dared to invade. It became a race for survival. In the chaos, Artemisia led her fleet to safety. During the escape, she noticed that one of the king's royal boats had been destroyed.

She spotted the body of the king's brother floating in the water and fished it out as she fled.

When they made it to safety, Artemisia presented Xerxes with the body of his brother so that he could give him a royal burial. Once again, Artemesia impressed Xerxes with her quick thinking.

He "rewarded" her by putting her in charge of getting two of his young sons—who had accompanied their father—back home safely.[14] There's no word on whether Artemisia thought this was a reward or a punishment, but for the Greeks, babysitting was recognizable as women's work.

She succeeded at that too, delivering Xerxes's sons to safety on Persian soil.

Meanwhile, the Greeks couldn't stand the idea that even

though they'd won, a woman admiral had outsmarted them. So they offered a reward of 10,000 drachmas—the equivalent of a boatload of silver—for her capture. Alive.

She outmaneuvered them there too. Although there is no record of how she evaded capture, we do know the queen happily continued ruling in Halicarnassus for years. Her family line led the kingdom for generations.

Lucky for us, her reputation as a brilliant admiral has never been capsized.

### Ancient Triple-Threat Battleships

Imagine a giant centipede with 200 stacked legs—short ones closest to the ground, middle ones atop those, and the longest reaching down from the top. All three rows of legs work in unison to move the creature in a super fast, though admittedly super creepy, way.

Now put that creature on the sea, and you have an idea what ancient battleships looked like. Called triremes, the "tri" is for the three banks of oars on every boat, which often required up to 200 men working their oars together, like some coordinated nightmare critter at sea.

Artemisia commanded five of these boats. The Persians had an estimated fleet of 1,300, compared to the Greeks, who had fewer than 400.

## So Why Did the Persians Lose?

The Greeks, unlike the Persians, were masters of the sea. They'd been building and sailing triremes for generations, while the Persians were experts at land warfare. The Persian fleets were manned by land fighters. We can imagine that a lot of them were in dire straits from being seasick on the journey over—especially after being battered by storms in the days and weeks before the big fight. In fact, many Persian ships were lost at sea.

Xerxes was likely pretty salty about those losses.

The Greek ships, on the other hand, were manned by not just trained sailors (no women allowed), but also by average citizens, including farmers, fishermen, tradesmen, and politicians. All of them rowed into sea battle together, fighting for their land, their people, and their freedom.

In other words, for the Greeks, it was win or die.

Both Greek and Persian ships featured metal-covered beaks that allowed ships to crash through enemy boats, thereby sinking them.

When the Persians encircled the Greeks, the Greek sailors reacted like cornered cats after a catnip binge—with lots of slashing, hissing, and spitting. Only with lots more severed body parts. In other words, it was mass chaos.

It was this massive level of crazy that also allowed Artemisia to trick her enemies by confusing them as to which side she fought on.

Her maneuvers saved her and her crew's lives.

And she impressed the Greeks so much, they immortalized her in their own stories of triumph!

## The Persian and Greek Gods

Though Artemisia fought for the Persians, it's likely that she and her people worshipped the Greek gods. After all, her city-state started out as a Greek colony. Plus, she was named after a Greek goddess.

The queen's Persian neighbors, though, likely worshipped a god named Ahura Mazda. Called Zoroastrianism for the ancient prophet Zoroaster, the ancient Persian faith is one of the world's oldest monotheistic religions.

According to Zoroastrian priests, or Magi, the god of fire and light gave humans the gift of free will. Life was a continuing struggle between good and evil. Fire represented goodness and the power of choosing light over darkness.

Many Persians worshipped other gods as well, including the sun god Mithras, who was said to have been born on December 25 and was sometimes known as the Unconquerable Sun. Mithras was also the god of friendship and treaties.

While Mithraism eventually died away, Zoroastrianism did not. Worshippers can still be found in small pockets of Iran today.

Belief in the Greek Olympians, on the other hand, disappeared with the ancient culture. And given the personalities of the Greek gods, it was probably a good thing.

## Fickle, Funny, and Frantic

Imagine a room full of unsupervised, sugared-up preschoolers. You'd find lots of tantrums, high-pitched screaming, and a shocking amount of hair-pulling.

Now supersize them, and you have the ancient Greek gods.

In the ancient world, gods behaving badly was not only accepted but celebrated: Zeus zapped anyone who questioned him, Hades stole a goddess to be his wife, Cronus ate his children, Hera tortured her husband's illegitimate kids, Athena started wars, Apollo chased a woman who turned into a tree to escape him, Aphrodite made terrible people fall in love just to watch them destroy each other . . . and that was just on a Monday!

The question, of course, is *why?* Why were the Greek gods so violent, mean, and unpredictable?

Many historians believe it's because ancient Greek *lives* were violent, mean, and unpredictable. The gods reflected the uncertainty and viciousness people faced every day: violence from nature in the form of storms and losses at sea, attacks from others in the form of wars, and passionate battles of will between people and families. Greek gods not only reflected the lives of the people, but promised a means of control too.

### "Here's the Deal, Zeus. I'll Sacrifice This Bull If You'll . . ."

Control came in the guise of sacrifices. Before you set off on a boat, you sacrificed a fish to Poseidon. Before a battle, you sacrificed a bull to Ares, the god of war.

In fact, you didn't dare make a move without giving the gods a little something. Sacrificing, or making gifts to the gods, was a major part of ancient religion. A sacrifice of any sort was like a request sent straight to Olympus: Please don't send a storm to sink my ship. Please don't send pestilence to ruin my crops. Please help me win this battle. Please make this person like me. Ancient religion was like an endless bargaining session with the unknown: I'll give you this, if you'll keep me safe or give me what I want.

And if you didn't get what you wanted—say, the crops *were* ruined, or you *lost* the battle—it meant that your gifts to the gods displeased them in some way. You just had to try harder next time. See? Control. Even if it was only an illusion, it made people feel better.

## "A God for You, a God for Me . . ."

The Greeks had gods for just about everything—food, wine, weather, marriage, love, sports, earthquakes, thieving, lying, shopping, animals, music, dancing, nature, and so on. By the time the Romans came along—they worshipped the same gods, only with Roman names—there were even gods of sewers.

We don't want to know what they sacrificed to them.

The most famous of the Greek gods, of course, were the twelve living it up atop a golden palace on a mountain in the sky named Olympus:

**Zeus:** The king of the gods had an electric personality. He wielded lightning bolts and got a charge from chasing women other than his wife. When he wasn't turning himself into an animal (bull, swan, eagle, etc.), he ruled over the sky, weather, law, order, justice, and fate.

**Poseidon:** God of the sea, rivers, floods, droughts, and earthquakes, Poseidon was like an angry sea monster with a taste for fish and ships. Greek sailors regularly sacrificed to this stormy god, hoping he wouldn't sink their boats. His animal was the horse, which he created in the racing sea-foam of violent waves.

**Hera:** Queen of the gods and the goddess of women,

marriage, and childbirth, her symbol was the hawk, or some-times a lion, which seemed fitting since she was always roaring about her husband Zeus's relationships with other women.

**Ares:** God of war, courage, and manliness, he sported a gleaming breastplate, a deadly gleam in his eye, and killer weapons. His taste for blood was alarming.

**Hermes:** God of thieves, messengers, roads, language, writing, athletic contests, travel, astronomy, and astrology, Hermes was like the junk drawer in the kitchen of the gods—he ruled over everything no one else cared about or wanted.

**Apollo:** Because the sun god ruled over poetry, prophecy, music, healing, and the arts, he thought he was hotter than any of the other gods. And maybe he was: he also pulled the sun across the sky on his golden chariot. He was often depicted with a lyre, an ancient stringed musical instrument.

**Demeter:** The goddess of agriculture, grain, bread, and the seasons, the mother of plants had a thorny temper. Her daughter Persephone was stolen by Hades, and she blighted the land with winter every year because she was angry. She's often shown holding a bouquet of wheat stalks.

**Athena:** The goddess of war, wisdom, weaving, and other arts and crafts, she's always depicted in armor, including a crested helmet and shield. She burst out of Zeus's head with helmet and battle gear in place, which must have left Dad with one heck of a headache.

**Hephaestus:** Ruler of fire, volcanoes, metalworking, stone building, and sculpture, this poor god was thrown out of Olympus by his own mother for being weak. Still, his creations were awesome, and he always carried blacksmithing tools around with him. Despite his fiery temper, he was supposed to be a sweet guy.

**Dionysus:** The god of wine, parties, vegetation, and fertility always carried an oversized goblet of wine and wore a crown of grape leaves. Everyone toasted the god of wine at the beginning of a celebration.

**Aphrodite:** If the goddess of love, beauty, and pleasure were a movie, she'd be a rom-com. She always made the wrong people fall in love and giggled in the shadows when it all went wrong.

**Artemis:** Goddess of the hunt, wildlife, and wilderness, she protected girls and women. She always carried a bow and arrow in case the hunting was good and had little patience for men who claimed to be better hunters.

Parents often named their children after gods—for example, Apollodorus for Apollo, Athenais for Athena, Demetra for Demeter, and so on. Guess who our heroine, Artemisia, was named after?

That's right—the fierce goddess of the hunt, Artemis. And like the huntress, she never backed down from a fight.

In an ironic twist, the Greeks built a sanctuary and temple to Artemis on the island of Salamis, thanking the goddess for her help in defeating Artemisia and Xerxes's Persian army. As the Persians slunk away in defeat, the Greeks celebrated Artemisia's very own namesake. Whether or not Artemisia found this amusing was not recorded.

### Were Amazons Real?

Artemisia's bravery and battle smarts captivated the ancient Greeks because they had a long history of being both fascinated and horrified by warrior women.[15]

But mostly horrified. Facing armed, powerful women

scared them more than a staring contest with Medusa.

So they came up with myths about a race of fierce warrior women from exotic lands who fought as bravely and as viciously as men. They called them Amazons. No story of a Greek hero was complete unless he wrangled—and defeated—an Amazon warrior. From Herakles (Hercules) to Theseus to Achilles, Greek heroes had to prove their worth by besting an Amazon. Greek legend even tells of a terrible attack on Athens by hordes of these warrior women.

Throughout most of history, people believed that the stories of Amazon warrior women were just that—stories. However, archaeology is proving that ancient warrior women existed. Multiple graves filled with the bones of battle-scarred women buried with weapons have been found all throughout the Eurasian steppes (today's Eastern Europe and Central Asia). Swords, daggers, shields, armor, bows and arrows, and slingstones have all been found buried near or on the bodies of young women.[16]

The nomadic, horse-riding people of the steppes still have a tradition of girls and young women hunting and fighting alongside boys and men.[17] To the Greeks, these no-nonsense, fearless female warriors were the stuff of nightmares. They integrated them into their stories and legends—making sure they were always defeated, of course—as a way of controlling their fears.

But real Amazonian warriors on horseback regularly trounced their enemies. Their descendants are still living today, defending their territories and hunting with eagles.

### Where "Power to the People" Began

Democracy comes from the Greek words for *people* and *power*. And until ancient Greeks thought to combine the concept with government, the world hadn't seen anything like it.

But democracy didn't just burst into existence one day. The idea of people voting for their own leaders and laws developed slowly over generations. Interestingly enough, it was the battle with Xerxes that proved the major catalyst for helping democracy take root in Athens.

See, after the Persians destroyed Athens, the Greeks became determined to rebuild their city better than ever. And that meant not just strengthening its walls but also empowering its citizens by giving them the right to vote.

For most of ancient history, groups of rich, powerful men or kings ruled. In the case of Sparta, they had *two* kings lest one fall in battle. In Athens, though, long before the Persian attacks, some brilliant politicians had begun creating laws that focused as much on protecting the weak as strengthening the strong.

Their focus was on creating a just and fair society—but only for property-owning men; the landless, women, and slaves were on their own.[18] Still, it was a start.

### Democracy and the Parthenon

Philosophy, theater, art, and science flourished under democracy. Most scholars call the era after the Persian wars the Golden Age of Athens. And nothing is more golden than the Acropolis, the famous temple of Athena built on a rocky outcrop overlooking the city.

The Parthenon was built on the ashes of temples the Persians had destroyed during Xerxes's invasion. Honoring the patron goddess of Athens, it housed a giant gilded statue of Athena, the Olympian protector of the city.

A marvel of architecture and beauty, the Parthenon

stood as a powerful symbol of Greece's triumph and spirit of endurance. It also became a symbol for the shining vision of democracy and equal representation under the law (but again, only if you were male and had property).

Even today, mostly in ruins, the Parthenon serves as *the* symbol for classical Greek and Athenian democracy. Its beautiful marble reminds us never to take democracy for *granite*.

## CHAPTER NOTES

[1]— Polyaenus, a Greek writer in the second century, wrote a book on war strategies of both Greeks and Romans. He unusually included a section on women leaders that includes Artemisia's victory by "cymbals" over arms.

Because we have no images of Artemisia during her lifetime, historians often refer to the statue of Artemis of Ephesus as an idealized guide for how she may have looked.

[2] — The Persian Empire had its heart in today's Iran. One source claims that as the kingdom expanded the king's title changed from the King of Kings of Iran to King of Kings of Iran and un-Iran.

[3] — Xerxes ruled over multiple regions that each spoke their own languages in what a leading scholar says was "without exaggeration, the greatest empire in the history of the world to date."

[4] — The Persian demand of "earth and water" was a way of making Persia's enemies acknowledge their superiority. It must have made the Greeks feel like mud.

[5] — Thermopylae, where the Spartans held off the Persians, was a narrow pass of "only fifty feet wide" at one point, with mountains on one side and the ocean on the other.

[6] — No one knows the exact numbers because ancient writers tended to exaggerate for effect. Herodotus, for example, claimed that the number of Persian soldiers was two million. Most scholars estimate that the Persians had anywhere from 80,000 to 300,000 Persians to 7,000 or 8,000 Greeks. One leading scholar believes the ratio of Persians to Greeks could've been as high as 20 to 1.

[7] — The Spartan king Leonidas and his famous 300 warriors died at Thermopylae. Herodotus claims Leonidas, like all his men, proved himself "extremely valiant."

[8] — "One of [Xerxes's] leaders was a woman: Artemisia, queen of the Greek city of Halicarnassus in Asia Minor and the lone female combatant among all the hundreds of thousands of men who followed Xerxes to Greece." Herodotus claimed, "Her ships were reputed to be the best in the whole fleet after the ships of Sidon . . ."

[9]— Historian Dr. Barry Strauss writes that the Persians had sent an insulting message: "Even a woman could fight the effeminate Greeks." They would eventually regret riling up their enemies in such a way!

[10]—The number of Persian fighters, says Strauss, comes from Herodotus and the Greek playwright, Aeschylus. He also points out that the massive armada was "followed by three thousand merchant vessels large and small, carrying food, supplies, and perhaps, spare towers."

[11]—Herodotus writes, "All those who were well disposed to Artemisia lamented her words." Too bad they didn't listen!

[12]—It is not clear if Xerxes understood that Artemisia had sunk an ally. Strauss conjectures that from his position, it may have looked like Artemisia had sunk a Greek ship instead.

[13]—Herodotus claims there was no point in mentioning any other commander and that he considered her "to be a great marvel."

[14]—Herodotus says Xerxes "commended" Artemisia and "sent her to Ephesus with his children."

[15]—Dr. Adrienne Mayor of Stanford University says, "The Greeks thought of Queen Artemisia I of Halicarnassus as a kind of maritime Amazon."

[16]—Amazons were not a myth. Archaeologists have discovered hundreds of graves of women warriors in Eurasia (today's Ukraine, Russia, and the steppes). They were buried with weapons, and most of their skeletons showed evidence of injuries consistent with battle wounds. Many of these young female warriors were teens!

Ancient writers claimed Xerxes gave Artemisia an alabaster jar of perfume as a thank you for her contributions at the Battle of Salamis. Because this jar bears his name and was found in the tomb of one of Artemisia's descendants, most scholars believe this is the one he gave her.

[17] — "The nomadic way of life, archery, and especially horses were the great equalizers for women . . . a horse-centered culture permitted parity of the sexes."

[18] — In Athens, these tools of democracy "served the people fairly well for almost two centuries."

# CHAPTER THREE

# AMANIRENAS

## THE ONE-EYED AFRICAN WARRIOR QUEEN

Once there was a fearless, one-eyed queen who stared down the most powerful man on the planet—and made him blink.

Her name was Amanirenas, and she ruled by the sword. In fact, that's how she lost her eye.

Amanirenas was queen of the powerful African kingdom of Kush in today's Sudan, south of Egypt.[1] This was the same land Hatshepsut conquered 1,400 years before Amanirenas's time. The queen ruled over a rich and vibrant land where women were respected and had power. Her people traded gold, wild animals, metals, ivory, ebony, oils, incense, and other goods with Egypt, Lebanon, Syria, Rome, Greece, and other Mediterranean nations.

During this period, Rome had replaced Xerxes and the Persians as the superpower of the ancient world, but it had challenges of its own. Four years before Amanirenas was born, Julius Caesar was assassinated by a bunch of backstabbing senators. When Amanirenas was just a kid, Caesar's successor declared war on another famous Egyptian queen, Cleopatra VII, and her husband, the Roman general Marc Antony.

Amanirenas and her people were probably very happy to see all that drama staying on Egypt's side of their shared border. Still, it's likely that she and her royal family watched the shenanigans between Rome and Egypt with a cautious eye, sharpening their swords and arrows just in case Rome got greedy and moved on them.

They didn't, at least for almost a decade. Then, without warning, Caesar's men took a stab at taking her lands.

But they'd messed with the wrong queen.

## A Nod to the Notable Nubians

Queen Amanirenas's region was called Kush, later called Nubia (for the purposes of this book, we will use *Nubia*). In general, her people belonged to a society identified as Meroitic.

The region had a long, rich history all its own, including a unique written language also called Meroitic.[2] Formed from Egyptian hieroglyphics, the code for Meroitic has still not been cracked, so there is much we don't know about the culture.

Hopefully, someone will figure it out soon!

As neighbors, the Nubians and Egyptians often acted like sisters who couldn't stand each other one moment but had each other's backs if outsiders threatened them.

Hatshepsut, pharaoh queen of the Eighteenth Dynasty, if you recall, invaded Nubia and ruled over it. Then Nubia kicked Egypt out but still maintained trade relations and strong cultural and religious ties with "big sister" Egypt.

A thousand years after Hatshepsut, the Nubians turned the tables and conquered Egypt. Known as the Twenty-fifth Dynasty, or the era of the Black Pharaohs, the Nubian kings and queens stabilized and strengthened Egypt. They also restored key religious sites and artifacts. But after ruling for nearly 100 years, the Nubians themselves were pushed out of Egypt by more invaders. At home, though, their kingdom flourished as they became the world's leading supplier of gold, iron, ivory, incense, and wild animals.[3]

Seven hundred years after Egypt's era of Black Pharaohs, Egypt fell again, but this time to the Romans. To add insult to injury, the Roman emperor Caesar Augustus claimed nearly all of Egypt as his own personal property. As in, just about the entire nation was his private backyard.[4]

Which only made his greedy friends pull out their shovels and dig hard for their share of treasure. Soon they cast their eyes south upon Nubia, their eyes dancing with visions of flashing coins. Think of all that gold! All that iron! All those spices and wild animals!

Without provocation, they attacked, taking five Nubian cities.

When Queen Amanirenas learned about the Roman attack, she likely had a very simple response: *Are you kidding me?*

## Queen on a Tear

The Romans must have assumed that the Nubians would not fight back. They left only the barest contingent of soldiers to hold the Nubian cities they'd conquered. Like a squirrel with a short attention span, the Roman general in charge of the assault scampered off to fight other battles.

While he was gone, Queen Amanirenas launched a surprise counterattack. She and her warriors trounced the Romans, and she snatched back all of her cities. For good measure, she wrecked several Roman military outposts too, fighting and winning against three Roman battalions.

In one of these skirmishes, the queen lost an eye. We have no details of the actual fight, but we can guess that despite her injury, she used her sword to take down her opponent before he could cut and run. The humiliated Romans, however, were on edge over their losses. They tried to make themselves feel better by accusing her of being "masculine" and, well, all-around terrifying.[5]

The queen didn't have time for their trash talk. She was too busy slashing to the heart of the matter: retaking her cities. After one battle, she gave the command to topple and behead all statues of the most powerful man in Rome, the emperor Caesar Augustus. She scooped up a bronze head of the emperor and marched home with it.

Then she buried the head under the entranceway to her palace temple. Why? So she could trample over his noggin several times day.

The message was clear: *Quit while you're ahead, Rome. Or more heads will roll.*

## A Royal Game of Cat and Mouse

Imagine how the Romans must have felt when they returned to their formerly conquered Nubian cities. Their soldiers had been beaten and many enslaved. Toppled headless statues of the emperor were everywhere. That woman had to be stopped!

A Roman general named Petronius went after her.[6] He recaptured her cities and went after the queen.

She evaded him.

Then when he wasn't looking, she swung around behind him and took her cities back *again.*

In the ensuing skirmishes, the Romans thought they had her beat several times. They were wrong. Amanirenas always snatched back her cities from right under their noses.

Finally, the Roman general threw up his hands in exasperation and in a rare meeting with the queen, said, *If you want Rome out of your business, you're going to have to talk to Caesar.*

This was the moment the queen left her enemy speechless.

*Who. Is. Caesar?* the bold, fearless queen asked.[7]

The Roman general's jaw must have dropped to the floor. How could anyone *not* know who the master of the world was?

After all, Rome ruled over a massive empire that included areas in what we call Italy, Spain, France, Germany, Greece, Bulgaria, Turkey, Algiers, Morocco, Libya, Syria, Lebanon, Israel, and Egypt.

Had she been pretending not to know who Caesar was? Or did she really not know? Either way, the message was clear: to Amanirenas and her people, Caesar was a *nobody*.

When the Roman left to report her comments to Caesar, we can imagine that her people sent him with plenty of aloe to treat the burn.

## We're Off to See the Caesar

Not sure how to handle such a stubborn opponent, the Romans sent for the queen to speak with the leader of Rome in person. Amanirenas and her crew were escorted by a Roman entourage to the Greek island of Samos to meet with Caesar Augustus.

The Romans did not record what happened when the queen met with the emperor, only that he treated her with great dignity and respect. It's fun to imagine, though, that she looked at him and made some quip about how his head was still attached to his body. You know, *un*like the head of his statue she'd buried under her walkway at home.

Whatever she said, she either charmed Caesar Augustus or let him know she would not be trifled with. According to historians, the emperor of Rome agreed to all of her demands.[8] Rome would withdraw from her cities. And her lands bordering Egypt would not have to pay taxes to Rome. Most importantly, Caesar promised never to invade her cities again.

For a so-called superpower, Rome sure submitted to all of the queen's terms pretty quickly! Remember, Rome almost never backed away from anyone. In terms of size and power differential, it was like a mouse squaring off against an elephant.

So how did the queen succeed in her mammoth smackdown?

Unfortunately, we only have the Roman version of the story, so it's mostly Roman historians making guesses. Some think that Caesar caved because he needed all his resources to focus on an upcoming war with Persia (ancient Iraq and Iran). Others wonder if maybe she threatened trade sanctions on the materials he needed so desperately—such as gold to pay his soldiers or iron to make their weapons. Just as likely, she'd impressed him with her fierce commitment to continue fighting Rome, no matter the cost.

We may never know.

But whatever she said, it convinced the emperor to back away slowly from her kingdom. And from her. Rome never dared to attempt to invade Nubian territory again.

After her victory, the one-eyed warrior queen returned to her palace and continued walking all over the emperor's tarnished bronze head, ruling strongly and wisely for years.

◉   ◉   ◉

### Plentiful Pyramids: Sudan Has More than Egypt

Egypt is famous for its ancient pyramids, but Sudan—the ancient center of the Nubian kingdom—has almost *twice* as many. About 200 pyramids dot the Nubian landscape versus 118 in Egypt.[9]

Nubian pyramids are narrower at the base than Egyptian pyramids and have steeper angles. The Nubians originally did not mummify their dead, but over time they absorbed Egyptian burial practices. Often the dead were placed on ceremonial beds and buried with treasures in chambers beneath their pyramids. Some even surrounded their beds with food, turning their eternal sleeping quarters into a sort of snack-filled knapsack.

The Nubians, like the Egyptians, also buried their dead surrounded by *shabtis*, small figures in the shape of mummies carved with spells written in hieroglyphics. In the afterworld, these figures would spring to life and do the dead's bidding—usually chores—so that the dead king or queen would not have to do them. When they were done cleaning, cooking, or hunting, the *shabtis* returned to their figurine form. It was like having a private maid service that never needed to be paid. Pretty sweet, right?

When it came to preparing for the afterlife, the Nubians and the Egyptians had every detail snugly wrapped up.

## Feats of Clay and First-String Warriors

Nubian artists often borrowed from Egyptian culture and vice versa, making the line between cultures a bit blurry. But when it came to pottery and gold, Nubian work shone brighter.

From polished black bowls to ceramics that mimicked complex weaving or featured geometric designs—likely crafted by women artisans—Nubian pottery has always been recognized for its beauty and practicality. However, Nubians really shone when it came to working with the metal that gave the region its greatest wealth: gold.

The region was famous for the artistry of its bracelets, earrings, pectorals, and other ornaments.[10] Queen Amanirenas was likely covered in gold jewelry in her tomb. Nubian jewelers were famed for their ornate and creative depictions of protective gods and goddesses.

## Thumbs-Up for the Bow Fighters

So expert were Nubia's archers that the Egyptians called Nubia the "Land of the Bow."[11] Thanks to their skill and accuracy, Nubian archers were hired as special units for armies throughout the ancient world. Nubian goddesses—as well as gods—often carried bows as a sign of strength, implying that women warriors also took up the weapon.

Nubians had a unique way of drawing a bow—with their thumbs rather than their forefingers—which allowed them to shoot with greater force and accuracy. Archers wore special thumb rings made out of stone, ivory, metal, or wood for protection.

It's unknown whether Queen Amanirenas fought with a bow and arrow, a sword, or both. Either way, we can guess that by the time she was through, her enemy was left *a-quiver*.

### Nubian Gods and Female Power

Egypt and Nubia shared a belief system. But like any pair of sisters, they each had individual personalities. For Nubia, that meant a greater emphasis on the majesty of lions and the power of strong queens.

Nubia's queens, like the lionesses that prowled their lands, ruled with impressive strength. And, as in a lion pride, the queens took charge, including, some believe, selecting the next king and queen. Amanirenas's daughter—Amanishakheto—ruled after her, indicating a formal mother-daughter succession.[12] All Nubian queens were given the title *kandake*, which means queen mother.

We don't know exactly how power was shared between Nubian queens and kings, but we can guess that either they shared it equally, or women took the lion's share.

### Lions Ruled in the Realm of the Gods Too

Lions were so important as symbols of strength and power to the Nubians that they combined their creator and war gods into one massively-maned god named Apedemak. This lion-god sometimes replaced the god Osiris to stand beside Isis and her son Horus. Apedemak was often depicted as a lion-headed, heavily muscled man carrying weapons, such as a bow or a sword, while smiting cowering enemies.

Temples to Apedemak abounded in Nubia. One hieroglyphic hymn from a temple wall describes him as he "who hurls his hot breath against the enemy . . . The one who punishes all who commit crimes against him. Who prepares a place for those who give themselves to him. Who gives to those who call to him. Lord of life, great in his sight."[13]

Statues of lions protected temples and guarded the lakes and reservoirs herders depended on for survival. Real lions were kept in some of the temples, fed and spoiled like giant house cats. Drawings on temple walls show the massive beasts sniffing lotus flowers and being serenaded by musicians.

Rams and ram-headed gods represented Amun, another creator-god who was often depicted as a man with ram horns. Presumably, they also kept rams in temples but likely not anywhere near the lions. After all, temples were for praying, not *prey*-ing.

### Supermama to the Rescue!

In ancient Egypt and Nubia, a goddess named Iset (more commonly known as Isis), was one of the most popular and powerful mother goddesses of all.[14] She resurrected her husband Osiris after his brother killed him and kept her son Horus alive through endless trials—proof that, even in ancient times, folks saved the drama for their mamas.

Isis was the goddess of magic and knowledge, a powerful and unbeatable combination. Both Egyptians and Nubians worshipped her as a supreme mother and ruler. Over time, Nubian queens were also associated with Nut, the goddess of air and the sky and mother to Isis, Osiris, and other major gods.

Whether goddesses or queens, clearly women totally ruled in Nubia.

## Nubians Used Antibiotics Long Before
## Anyone Knew about Germs

Long before humans ever heard of germs, the Nubians figured out that brewing a special yeast in their beer provided great protection against sickness. That yeast was actually a type of antibiotic, medicine that kills bacteria. Modern antibiotics, such as penicillin, have saved countless lives.

Archaeologists studying Nubian remains were puzzled by proof of tetracycline—a type of antibiotic—present in the bones of mummified Nubian grown-ups and children alike. How, they wondered, was that possible? Antibiotics were a modern invention, weren't they?

It turns out the ancient Nubians used the grains and brewed the yeast that make up the essential properties of antibiotics in their beer. They didn't call it that, but it worked just the same. From childhood on, Nubians drank this special beer, which protected them from life-threatening bacterial infections.[15]

Most people in ancient societies—including children—drank diluted beer or wine. Experts guess that ancient healers observed fewer tummy aches in patients who drank alcohol versus those who drank plain water. They didn't know about bugs or germs, of course, but they somehow made the connection. It is likely that the alcohol in fermented drinks destroyed many of the bugs that made people sick.

Nubia's special antibiotic beer had extra healing properties. And, scientists say, their concoction had a lovely blue-green tinge to it, which likely added to the perception of "magic" medicine.

Given the effectiveness of antibiotics on many bacterial

diseases, Nubian healers must have been highly respected throughout the region. After all, their special beer cured what *ale-d* people!

❖

## CHAPTER NOTES

[1] — Ancient Nubia spanned the "northern part of the modern state of Sudan and the southernmost part of Egypt."

[2] — Meroitic writing was a mix of hieroglyphics and cursive. "Linguists have attempted to classify the Meroitic language, but such attempts have proved futile." In other words, no one has cracked the code . . . *yet*.

Nubian queens, called kandakes, were powerful rulers. We have no images of Amanirenas; this is her descendant, Queen Amanitore.

[3] — Think animals for gladiator shows and metals for war. Nubia also exported "ostrich feathers, gold, ivory, leopard skins." Its economic success depended on its iron industry and gold mining.

[4] — Augustus took ownership of most of Egypt after defeating Antony and Cleopatra—in other words, he claimed most of the land as his "personal estates." Why? Because he could!

[5] — Ancient Greek historian Strabo, who was alive during Amanirenas's skirmishes with Rome, is the one who tried to throw shade by describing the queen as a "masculine woman" who had "lost an eye."

[6] — The first Roman general to attack the queen's cities was a man named Gallus, who may have planned to continue sacking Amanirenas's cities but was called away by Rome to fight in Arabia.

This bronze head of Augustus was found buried under the queen's palace; many scholars believe this is the trophy Amanirenas took after snatching her cities back from the Romans.

[7]— Strabo claimed that when they asserted "that they did not know who Caesar was, nor where they were to find him," the Roman general gave them escorts and took them to Caesar in Samos.

[8]— Strabo wrote that Amanirenas and her "ambassadors obtained all that they desired, and Caesar even remitted the tribute he had imposed." In other words, he gave back the riches the Romans had taken from her queendom!

[9]— It was only in 2011 that the Nubian pyramids were finally listed as UNESCO World Heritage Sites.

[10]—"Nubia was known for its exotic luxury goods— especially gold," reported the Boston Museum of Fine Arts, host to the exhibit "Gold and the Gods: Jewels of Ancient Nubia."

Nubia was the leading exporter of gold in the ancient world. Its artisans were renowned for their work.

[11]—The name, "Land of the Bow," was initially imposed
upon Nubians by ancient Egypt.

[12]—According to Nubian scholars, Amanirenas's daughter
ruled after her death and built one of the largest palaces
found in the region to date.

[13]—The Nubians took great pride in their main lion
god. They carved Apedemak's inscription/prayer in
hieroglyphics at the lion temple at Musawwarat-es-Sufra.

[14]—To the ancient Egyptians, Isis was a powerful goddess
of magic and protection, but her name unfortunately
became synonymous with a terrorist organization, the
Islamic State of Iraq and Syria. Many people in North
America and around the world have asked the media to
stop using that term to try to cut the association with the
ancient goddess.

[15]—The ancient Nubians didn't call their special beer
"antibiotics," of course, because there was no such
word or concept. They just knew their brew made
everyone healthy and *hop-py*!

## CHAPTER FOUR

# THE TRUNG SISTERS

## A QUEEN AND HER SISTER TAKE ON A TITAN

Around the same time that the Romans began tromping through the West, two sisters in the East, Trung Trac and Trung Nhi, stood up to invaders who threatened their land and people. The sisters faced Chinese invaders who, like the Romans, were the military superpower of the Asian continent.

The Chinese had taken over the region during the Han Dynasty and set their sights on southern China and what we call northern Vietnam today.[1]

Only one problem: the Trungs and their people were already there and thriving socially, economically, and culturally. The Vietnamese (although not yet named as such) did not want or need Chinese overlords, thank you very much. They had a rich, self-sufficient culture where women were respected and empowered.[2] They grew rice in the Red River valley and traded goods successfully with regional neighbors.

But like bookworms let loose in a brand new library, their northern neighbor—China—wanted all the bestsellers for itself. The Chinese conquered the region in 111 BCE, but the locals did not close the book on independence yet.

## Sisters in Crime

One hundred fifty years into the occupation, one Chinese over-lord grew too greedy for his own good. He taxed the people on not just everything they grew but also everything they touched—including salt. And when that wasn't enough, he taxed the fish caught in the locals' very own rivers.[3]

They had to pay a tax on fish they caught in their own water? The people were gutted. And furious.

So a local leader asked the Chinese leader to back off. The official's response? *Kill him.* The greedy governor had the local man murdered.

The executed man just happened to be Trung Trac's husband. And she had a sister named Trung Nhi.

The Chinese overlord had messed with the wrong women. These powerful, land-owning sisters would be pushed no further.

The newly widowed Trung Trac demanded retribution. The Chinese ignored her. So she and her sister did the only reasonable

thing: *they raised an army of 80,000 soldiers.*

Unfortunately, we have no accounts of how the sisters convinced so many locals to fight back, but whatever they said, it worked. Men and women, farmers and fishermen, old and young—came together to back the sisters in their bid for independence.

Trung Trac and Trung Nhi led the charge against the Chinese, fighting on elephants. Their elderly mother commanded as general.

The stampede was on.

## From Warriors to Queens

While the corrupt Chinese overlord ran—it was rumored he'd shaved his head so he could cross back into China unrecognized—the Trungs' forces took over formerly Chinese military outposts and government centers. The movement grew. Local lords sent additional fighters. Eventually the Trung sisters took more than sixty-five strongholds, pushing the Chinese up and out.[4]

And even after the Chinese governor had run for his life back to his own country, no replacement appeared on the horizon.

The Trung sisters had done it. They'd liberated their people. Everyone rejoiced. But then the people looked around and wondered, *Now what?*

Who would lead them? Who would make the decisions to keep the economy going and the people working?

*Relax,* the sisters insisted. *We got this.*

## The Queens of Means

*A woman proudly led a young nation;*
*Even the Han emperor heard of it and was terrified.*

—Seventeenth Century Poet, Dang Thanh Le

All of the sixty-five formerly Chinese-held strongholds—spanning from the southernmost region (today's central Vietnam) to regions in the north (today's southern China)—bent a knee toward the sisters. Trung Trac was named their queen. And Trung Nhi ruled as deputy queen.

Clearly, two queens were better than one. The sisters proved that girl power was even better when it was double-teamed.

While the Chinese may have found rule by queens shocking, the locals did not. Long before they were invaded and overtaken, they lived in a matriarchal society, which means power was handed down via the mother's bloodline. Women had political and economic power. They could work, own property, and accumulate wealth.[5]

Queen Trung Trac quickly set things to rights by removing burdensome Chinese taxes. The common folk could finally breathe easy. Traditional lines of property ownership, hereditary rights, and farming practices were reinstated. Everyone, it seemed, was happy.

But the queens also knew that China was like the big, bad wolf just waiting to attack. Unfortunately, they had no idea just how big, bad, and angry that wolf had grown.

Nor how determined it had become to make its enemies howl in pain.

## "I'll Huff, and I'll Puff, and I'll BLOW Your House Down . . ."

While the Trung sisters stabilized the region, the Chinese were busy stalking their newly independent prey. And nearly two and a half years after the queens' victory, the big, bad wolf finally headed south to reclaim what the Trung sisters had taken back. Unfortunately for the sisters, the wolf-pack leader was a Chinese general famous for his harsh fighting style. The Chinese called him the Wave-Calming General.[6]

He should've been dubbed the Tsunami of Death. After all, he marched in with a force of 20,000 highly disciplined fighting men. It was only a matter of time before the Trung sisters and their people were in over their heads.

Although we have no numbers, scholars guess that the Trung sisters didn't have as much success in raising an army this time. After all, the mood had changed. Locals had returned to their families and their farms, fishing boats, and villages. Few were interested in fighting again.

Still the sisters prepared the best they could. They reminded their people that they were fighting for their way of life, their pride, and their independence.

But as the professional killing machine known as the Chinese army marched on, many locals were intimidated. They began to question the sisters' leadership. Yes, their people had a long history of strong ruling women, but after 150 years of Chinese occupation—when women were devalued—not everyone felt comfortable with the queens in charge. This led to infighting. Some of the people ran. Others went to the Chinese side.

But not the tough Trungs. Despite their diminished support, for them it was independence or die.

## The Battle Royale

The matchup between the local people and the Chinese was unequal to the extreme. Just as before, the Trungs' army consisted of average folk—men and women who farmed, fished, and lived simple lives. The Chinese army, on the other hand, was made up of highly trained professional warriors.

Imagine if the Super Bowl–winning football team took on the local high school junior varsity team. You could root for the young, brave, idealistic team all you wanted, but it would be just a matter of time before the bigger team cleated their bones into the ground.

Still the Trung sisters refused to give up hope. Near the site of today's Hanoi, they fought heroically on elephants, wielding shining swords alongside many female generals who'd also committed to fight unto death. Sadly, it wasn't enough.

## Overrun, but Not Overcome

The fighting continued even as it became clear their battle for independence was a lost cause. Legend tells of one heavily pregnant general who went into labor during battle.[7] Surrounded by her warriors, she gave birth, and like Rafiki holding Simba aloft on Pride Rock, she raised her child to the sky then wrapped it on her back and resumed fighting. With a sword in each hand, she began to carve her way through the enemy to safety, but when it became clear that her troops could not hold the Chinese off, she threw herself and her newborn into the river rather than be caught and tortured by the enemy.

Meanwhile, the Trung sisters fled south as the Chinese "Tsunami of Death" surged over their lands. They'd lost. And it must have been soul crushing. Despite their best efforts, they had lost their freedom, their power, and their ancient traditions—not to mention the lives of countless friends and compatriots.

Still, according to local legend, the queens refused to be captured. They climbed up a steep cliff, and with heads held high, together they threw themselves into a river and drowned.

The Chinese could take their land, but they would never take the sisters alive. The sisters made sure of that with one last act of defiance.

The victors, of course, had a different version of the sisters' demise. The Chinese claimed that they captured the queens, had them beheaded, and sent their heads to the emperor in central China.[8]

We can only presume they told the story to get *a-head* of any future rebellions.

However the queens died, the Vietnamese people never forgot the dedication and fierceness of the sisters, even as Chinese rule continued for another 900 years. The spirit of the fearless Trungs continued to live on, even into the twentieth-century war of independence against France. To this day, the sister queens are honored by memorials in temples dedicated to them, the biggest of which resides in the city of Hanoi.

The lives and legends of the proud sisters who would not bend still stand tall in the hearts of the Vietnamese.

### Grabbing a Tiger by the Tail

Not only were the Trung sisters fierce leaders, but they also hunted tigers in their spare time.

According to legend, a man-eating tiger had been terrorizing the countryside around the time the Trung sisters came to power.[9] To prove their worth and ability as leaders, the sisters hunted and skinned the fearsome beast. Trung Nhi wore the tiger's pelt as a cape. But before doing so, she added a gruesome touch, writing down a proclamation on the inside of the tiger's skin, detailing all the reasons the people needed to unite to overthrow their Chinese overlords.

It worked. The people came together. Proving that the Trungs' instincts for inspiring a fighting spirit were . . . well, *grrreat!*

## The Dragon and Fairy:
## Mythic Origins of Vietnam

The Vietnamese call themselves "children of the dragon and grandchildren of the fairy" thanks to an ancient legend about their origins.[10]

Long ago, a gleaming dragon emerged from the sea and dragged himself up on land. Abundant and beautiful, the land welcomed him. At the same time, a fairy glided down from the mist-covered mountains. She too was swept away by the land's beauty and lushness.

One day, the dragon and the fairy met and came together. The fairy gave birth to 100 children. While the two immortals were happy together, they knew it could not last. The dragon had to return to the sea, and the fairy longed for her home in the high mountains. The dragon took fifty of the children and the fairy the remaining fifty, and they parted. Thus, the 100 descendants of the dragon and fairy split up the land—those who lived by the sea and those who made their homes in the mountains. Although sometimes they fought, they recognized that they were of the same people and often came together to fight invaders from other lands.

They may have lived apart, but when they banded together, the children of the dragon ruled.


## From Top to Bottom:
## How Confucianism Punted Women
## Out of Power

Long before the Chinese invaded from the north, the people of Vietnam respected women as leaders, both in the family and in the community. However, the invading Chinese brought with them a philosophy and political system called

Confucianism, which placed women at the bottom of society.

Confucius lived in China in the fifth century BCE. While his teaching stressed kindness, ethical behavior, and respect, it also taught that women had to stay quiet, tend children, and keep out of government.[11]

We can assume that didn't go over so great with the ancestors of the Trung sisters.

## "What Do You Mean We Have to Stand in the Back?"

Many scholars believe that before the Chinese invasion, the local culture valued women as equals. The Trung sisters' rebellion was likely the last gasp of a culture where women's wisdom and leadership abilities were respected and followed.

To have local women not only take control of armies but also succeed in pushing them out must have shocked and dismayed the Chinese. Their egos were likely insulted, which is why they amassed the most powerful army they could muster—under the rule of the most ruthless general of his time—to quash the rebellion.

For the 900 years they ruled afterward, the Trungs' conquerors likely wished everyone would forget about the brave women who ran them off for a time. Fortunately for us, no one did.

## Two Hundred Years after the Trungs, Another Warrior Queen Attacked

Still ruled by the Chinese—this time under the Kingdom of Wu in third century CE—the Vietnamese once again faced terrible abuses. And once again, a strong woman fought for their rights. Her name was Ba Trieu, which means "Lady Trieu."

At only nineteen, she fled for the hills and amassed a large and powerful rebel army. Her older brother, it was said, tried to talk her out of fighting the powerful Chinese. She famously responded:

*I want to ride the stormy sea, subdue its treacherous waves, hunt sharks in the open sea, drive out the aggressors and repossess our land, undo the ties of tyranny and never bend my back to be the concubine of any man.*[12]

You've got to admit, this teen had a way with words.

But she was a woman of action too. She mounted a war elephant and led her forces. Lady Trieu won thirty battles against the Chinese and succeeded in creating a safe buffer zone.

According to legend, she had an additional buffer all her own too—her breasts were said to be three or four feet long! To fight, she either threw them over her shoulders or tied them down under her armor. There's not a lot of . . . er, *support* for that legend, though.[13]

But, like the Trung Sisters, her forces were eventually squashed. Also like the sisters, she refused to be captured and threw herself into the river.

But how she sacrificed herself was *ir-elephant.* Her bravery and heroism was what made her stand out.

She too, along with the Trungs, is honored today in temples throughout the region.

❖

## CHAPTER NOTES

NOTE: For ease of reading and out of respect for the intricacies of Vietnamese diacritics, the names in this chapter were anglicized. Thank you to Dr. C. Giebel and Tam Hoang for consultations on the issue.

[1] — The Chinese invasion southward was relentless and eventually eroded all resistance.

[2] — The native (pre-Vietnamese) population had a tradition of "greater freedom allowed to women. Daughters as well as sons could own and inherit land and serve as trustees of their ancestral cult funds."

There are no ancient images of the Trung sisters, but their stories continue to inspire artists.

[3] — The locals were taxed even for fishing in their own rivers!

[4] — Trung Trac had a knack for strategy—she gave the orders to take out military barracks and police stations first, which made it harder for the enemy to regroup and fight back.

[5] — "Ancient Vietnamese society may not have been controlled by women, but it is clear that women enjoyed hereditary rights that allowed them to assume roles of political leadership."

[6] — The Wave-Calming General had a long track record of drowning any opposition to Chinese rule.

[7] — The legend of the woman who gave birth while fighting (her name was Phung Thi Chinh), who continued fighting unto death, was a testament to the strength and commitment of the native people.

[8] — Embarrassed by almost being taken down by women, the Chinese spread word that they'd killed Trung Trac and Trung Nhi. They wanted to keep the sisters from being turned into heroes. It didn't work.

[9] — The tiger story is considered a "colorful legend."

[10] — The legend of the marriage between the dragon king from the sea (the coast) and a fairy from the bird kingdom (the mountains) is an integral part of Vietnamese culture, according to Dr. Chonchirdsin of the Centre for South East Asian Studies at the University of London.

[11] — Confucianism was heavily patriarchal and clashed with the pre-Vietnamese tradition of respect for women.

[12] — Lady Trieu supposedly uttered this smackdown in the third century CE.

[13] —To us, the story of Lady Trieu throwing her three-foot-long breasts over her shoulders sounds silly and vaguely insulting, but we can't assume the ancients saw it that way—it could very well be that they were honoring her femininity with this tale.

Dragons played a huge mythic role in the region and can be found decorating many Vietnamese buildings and temples.

## CHAPTER FIVE

# BOUDICCA

## BIG, BAD, AND MAD

Tall and powerful, the tribal Queen Boudicca had long red hair that whipped in the wind like ropes dipped in blood. She drove a chariot with the fury of a goddess chasing storm clouds across the sky. Her battle cry made beasts run for cover. And when she raised her strong arms to invoke the gods of war, her enemies trembled with awe.

Her name was Boudicca (*Boo*-dee-kah), and she led a rebellion against the most powerful war machine of its time—the Roman army.

Thanks to Boudicca, Rome nearly called it quits in Britannia (ancient Britain). Boudicca's forces annihilated an entire Roman legion and razed several Roman cities and strongholds. Despite Rome's strength and superpower status, she came close to pushing the pushy world conquerors all the way out of her isle.

The Romans had never seen anyone like her.

## The Woman Who Terrified Rome

Boudicca was queen of a tribe of Celts (pronounced with a *k* sound—that's right, we've been pronouncing the Boston Celtics incorrectly all this time!). She ruled a tribe called the Iceni in eastern Britain in 60 CE. As many as thirty to fifty Celtic tribes coexisted at the time—though not always peacefully—on the British Isles. Boudicca and her tribe burst onto the pages of history after one of Rome's biggest boneheaded blunders—greed and stupidity so big, it boggled the mind even then.

The Iceni were originally fairly accepting of Romans on their island. Julius Caesar, one of the most fearsome and successful generals in Rome's history, invaded Britain in 55 BCE in search of pearls.[1] For real. Caesar *shellfish-ly* thought he could get rich by taking all the little sea jewels from the "strange isle" across the sea.

He also wanted the land's gold and other metals mined in the region. But he quickly wished he'd stabbed that idea in the back—especially after the wild-haired, blue-painted, naked warriors of the British Isles pushed back.

After two tries, Caesar tossed his plans—and presumably his salad on the ship ride home—and left for good.

After the Roman general left, the Iceni likely never gave much further thought to Caesar and his pearl hunters.

Nearly eighty years later, though, another Roman leader sailed for Britannia, an emperor named Claudius. He figured winning a victory in the island that had pushed out the great Julius Caesar seemed like a nice way to start his reign.[2] And he was right. When Boudicca was just a child, the Romans settled in and took over for good.

Boudicca's tribe did not challenge the Romans initially. After all, the Iceni lived on the far eastern end of Britain. Their lands were vast and secluded and were not near Roman settlements. The Iceni were too busy farming, trading, raising hunting dogs, breeding horses, and warring with neighboring tribes over hunting rights to bother much with the Romans. From the beginning, they agreed to cooperate as long as the Romans left them alone.

And for a while, they did.

But as Roman settlements grew, so did Roman greed. Eventually Rome demanded loyalty from all of the Celtic tribal kings. After witnessing Rome annihilate those who tried to defy them, Boudicca's tribe wisely agreed, as did many other native leaders.

Still, Boudicca and the Iceni likely never completely trusted the well-armed invaders. They enjoyed an uneasy kind of peace with Rome, kind of like mice sharing a room with a big fat cat.

## "Hey, Who Stole My Cheese?"

As the years passed and Boudicca's husband became king of the

Iceni, Rome demanded more and more from the native British tribes. Some rebelled, but not Boudicca's people. They did whatever the Romans demanded to keep the peace. In exchange, the Iceni earned some extra privileges.

Like *staying alive*, for one. The tribes that fought against Rome didn't last long.

It was a good strategy.

Until Boudicca's husband died. To keep the peace and protect the tribe, the Iceni king left a will giving the Roman emperor *half* his kingdom. He hoped Rome would see it as a gift and leave his people alone. The other half of his kingdom he gave to his two daughters. Boudicca, as his queen, would rule until their girls were old enough to take over.[3]

Pretty generous, right? The rats gave away half their cheese. But the cat pounced anyway and demanded the whole thing.

## "Oh No, They Didn't!"

First, Roman soldiers stomped into Boudicca's village and took everything they owned—money, food, jewelry, horses, etc. They even made everyone give up their weapons. But Boudicca's people, like most Celts, were proud warriors. Turning over their weapons was like ripping out their hearts![4]

The queen got up in the face of the Romans stealing all their goods. They couldn't do that! They had cooperated with the Romans. And her husband had given them half of everything they owned. How dare they act this way!

The Romans sneered. Half wasn't good enough. They wanted everything. When Boudicca refused to back down, the Roman in charge gave the order: drag her into the village center and whip her. Worse, he did nothing to stop his thugs from attacking Boudicca's daughters, leaving the teens barely alive.

Rome's mistreatment of Boudicca, her daughters, and her people was beyond imaginable. Why mess with a powerful tribe that was on your side? There was no explaining their cruelty. But based on what Boudicca did next, we can guess that she figured there was no forgiving it either.

The Romans would pay.

## Beware an Angry Celtic War Goddess

Boudicca wasn't just a queen. It's likely that she was a priestess too. Celtic religion was called druidism. Druids were the priestly class of Celts—the ones in charge of religious practices.

In Celtic/druid societies, women ruled alongside men. Women also fought during wartime and led religious rites. The Romans thought the Celts' respect for women was crazy.[5] To Romans, a good woman stayed behind the scenes. Sure, she could wield *some* power, but only as long as it wasn't in your face.

But to Boudicca, a good woman loudly and proudly took care of her people and fought against injustice.

Unfortunately, the Romans blamed the druids for the locals' defiant attitudes. So they went after their religious center—a sacred isle named Mona—attacking innocent priests and priestesses and torching the Celts' sacred groves.

Usually Romans respected other faiths. Not so in Britain. The Roman policy for the ancient Brits wasn't toleration, but elimination. Sadly, the religion never recovered after Rome's attack. Druid mysteries, practices, and legends died at the hands of Rome's army.[6]

But while the Romans trampled their faith, Boudicca went into action. First she unified nearly all of the major tribes in her region—close to half of the tribes on the whole island, something no one else had been able to do before or since. Then she planned her attack. First up? The symbols of Roman occupation: the cities that the Romans built for themselves.

Amazingly, the Romans never saw it coming.

## Attack!

With Boudicca in charge, the Celts attacked the city of Camulodunum, today's Colchester. Ten thousand angry Brits swarmed the colony of retired Roman soldiers, their families, and slaves (mostly Celts captured in earlier rebellions).

Before they arrived, the panicked vets of the Roman city sent a message to the Roman guy who started the whole mess. You remember him—the one who gave the order to steal all the Icenis' stuff, and have Boudicca whipped and her daughters attacked.

*Help!* they begged. *They're out for revenge. Send reinforcements!*

But like the spineless worm he was, he sent just 200 men and then slithered off the island. He stole away by boat, never to be heard from again.[7]

Out for blood, Boudicca and her army of enraged, blue-painted naked warriors swarmed the city. Even with the reinforcements, the Romans didn't stand a chance. Boudicca and her people overpowered all of them. They freed the slaves, most of whom joined her army. They attacked every home, store, and temple. They looted the city for weapons and food and then burned it to the ground.

Nobody, not a single Roman, made it out alive.

They left nothing but a smoldering mound of rubble.

## An Unstoppable Legion—Stopped

Word of the rebellion reached the Roman general, a guy named Paulinus, interrupting his massacre of the druids. A rebellion led by a mere queen? No problem. He continued hacking away at their sacred religious center and sent his legion to take care of the nuisance.

The plan was to cut her off at the pass between the city she attacked and her next destination—Londinium (today's London). The Ninth Legion—more than 5,000 warriors—marched twenty-five miles a day toward the rebellion. They slogged through the damp woods, expecting a formal battle. They never anticipated the way the blue-painted Celts melted into the mist.

In a surprise ambush, Boudicca caught the Romans unprepared and cut them down. Every soldier marching on foot died. Only a handful of the cavalry—the men who fought on horses—made it out alive.

Boudicca had accomplished the impossible: she'd destroyed an entire Roman legion.

## Londinium is Falling Down, Falling Down . . .

Chariot-riding Boudicca was on a roll. When the Roman general Paulinus received word of his legion's loss, he finally paid attention. He and an elite group of fighters hightailed it to Londinium, guessing that it was next on Boudicca's take-out menu. He was right.

Driving his men and horses hard, Paulinus got to London before Boudicca and her forces arrived. He intended to protect the center of Roman trading. But after one look at the unfortified town, he changed his mind.

He spread the word: *Everybody out. We can't protect you, so you might as well run.* Then he turned and marched out of the city. Those with money escaped right away; the rest were on their own.

Nice, huh?

But Boudicca was no kinder. Her army slaughtered everybody left in the city, tens of thousands of civilians, and burned the entire city to the ground. Londinium burned so hot, the city melted into a thick layer of red clay. You can still see this layer of destruction today, thirteen feet below London's streets, as archaeologists dig for more information on Boudicca's attack.[8]

## The Sting of Queen "B"

The Romans just couldn't wrap their heads around the idea of a successful woman-led army. They called her a crazy wild woman and her army an unruly mob. But not modern historians. They recognize that she controlled her troops with excellent "skill and generalship."[9] Plus she was no hothead; she showed great patience. She could have gone berserk over the mistreatment of her daughters and attacked right away. But she didn't. She took her time, gathering support from many British tribes to strengthen her forces.

Still, she made one fatal error.

After the Celts' victory at Londinium, Boudicca marched toward a third Roman city to turn that one into toast too. But she should've gone after General Paulinus instead.

Remember, Paulinus had left Londinium and all its citizens to die at her hands because he didn't have enough troops to fight her. As Boudicca's warriors roasted marshmallows over the burning embers of her latest conquest, Paulinus gathered every Roman fighter he could find. He even called for backup from troops in ancient France.

He wasn't taking any more chances with the killer queen.

If only the queen had attacked the Roman general before

he had time to regroup, British history might have been entirely different. Most scholars think Rome would've called it quits and pulled out of ancient Britain altogether.

But it didn't work out that way. Instead, Boudicca and her army faced a final Roman surprise.

## The Last Stand

Paulinus set a trap. He attacked British religious sites in the area, knowing that it would bring the Brits buzzing to him like bees around a hive. As expected, Boudicca made a beeline for him.

The result? Paulinus and his soldiers controlled the battleground. He chose an area in Middle Earth . . . er, the British Midlands that was mostly open field. A dense forest covered their backs, and steep slopes protected their sides.

Now the Romans could contain the larger British forces. The natural barriers meant that Boudicca's army couldn't surround the Romans and overwhelm them with their greater numbers. They were penned on three sides, and they didn't even know it.

Then the Celts made one big mistake. And it sealed their fate.

## That's How We Roll!

The Celts were so sure they'd be dancing around a victory bonfire that night, they could almost smell the smoke. After all, they seriously outnumbered the Romans. Plus, they had the home-field advantage. Or so they thought.

To get a close view of the slaughter, the Celts who weren't fighting rolled their wagons behind their warriors to cheer them on. Women with babies in their arms, young children, and the elderly chanted for blood.

Just an everyday picnic on wheels, right? Unfortunately, they didn't realize that their wagons created the fourth side of the trap, boxing their own army in the center.

In her prefight speech, Boudicca claimed that she was fighting for her "lost freedom, my bruised body, and my outraged daughters." Then she asked each and every fighter what they were fighting for. They roared, answering that they fought for "independence and self-rule."

As priestess of her people, Boudicca also performed a religious rite during her speech. With great pomp, she released a hare from inside her robe. The creature immediately bounded to freedom. It was a "sign from the gods," she claimed—like the hare, all of the British tribes would finally be free of Rome too. The Celts were about to have a great *hare* day![10]

Boudicca whipped her forces into a frenzy. With a roar, she commanded everyone—men, women, and anyone who could hold a weapon—to "Fight to win or die!"

But the battle didn't go as planned. The steely, disciplined Romans held their positions even as the Celts taunted and threw rocks and spears at them. Their long shields protected their bodies. Their cold eyes stared out from gleaming helmets.

The Romans launched 7,000 javelins all at once into the

screaming horde of Celts. The coordinated attack caused chaos for the free-wheeling Celts. Another Roman javelin assault immediately followed.

With guttural screams, the blue-painted horde of Celts came at the Romans with their long swords—weapons that could split a man in two. But you needed room to swing these supersized weapons, and the Romans didn't give them any. They pressed forward, crowding the Celts into a mass of helpless, squirming bodies. Then they pushed them back against their own sightseeing wagons at their rear. The Celts were trapped. And the slaughter began for real.

The Roman army's reputation as an efficient killing machine was proven that day. Just about every Celtic man, woman, and child was killed. Blood drenched the fields and woods.

Boudicca and her two daughters somehow escaped. But rather than die at the hands of their enemies, they took poison. The queen's body has never been found.[11]

## What Happened to the Celts?

The Romans were furious with the Celts for daring to fight for independence, but they were even more furious with *themselves* for almost losing to a woman. They were determined to teach the Celts a lesson.

So General Paulinus put the hurt on everything in his path. He killed Celts wherever he turned and enslaved countless more. He even beat up their dirt. Yes, that's right, dirt. He wrecked some of their farming soil so they couldn't grow anything.

That's when the big bosses in Rome stepped in. If the Celts couldn't farm, then they couldn't eat. And if they couldn't eat, then they couldn't mine for gold, pay taxes, or send Rome money. And wasn't that why they invaded Britain in the first place?

So the emperor pulled the plug on the general. Paulinus went back to wherever he came from, and in came a new Roman general and ruler. Thankfully, the new guy knew how to "play nice." He showed the Celts respect. He rebuilt relationships with the local tribes.

The Romans ended up ruling Britain for another several hundred years—right up until they left the island for good around 410 CE, about 100 years before the Middle Ages (around 500 to 1500 CE).

Still, Boudicca's reputation lived on. The warrior queen of Britain eventually became the country's first national heroine. Boudicca meant *victory*, which later morphed into the name Victoria.

Almost 2,000 years later, another British queen ruled the land. And she was named after Boudicca—Queen Victoria. This British "victory queen" ended up ruling an empire even larger than Rome's.

Boudicca would've loved that. A queen bearing her name ruled unchallenged at last!

## Lifting the Kilt on Boudicca's People

What do kilts, friendship rings, and the NBA's Boston Celtics all have in common? They're all connected to the Celts, Boudicca's ancient people.

The original Celts were a warlike people that swarmed over today's Germany, France, Belgium, and northen Italy. Eventually, the Celts also settled in what we call England, Ireland, Wales, and Scotland hundreds of years before the Greeks fought Xerxes (see Chapter Two, "Artemisia"). And you won't believe how we know about their culture: from ancient philosophers such as Aristotle and even the Roman general Julius Caesar, who took on the Celts in many battles.[12] Other ancient Greek and Roman observers also clued us in to the lives of the Celts:

- Celts did not consider themselves a single "people." They had more tribes and splintering of tribes than McDonald's has branches.
- They were head and shoulders above most of their enemies—literally. They often towered over their shorter Greek and Roman rivals. There is a famous story of Alexander the Great meeting with the Celts on one of his campaigns. "What do you fear the most?" Alexander asked, hoping they'd say, "You, O great conqueror." Instead they said that the "sky might fall upon" us. You know, because they were so *tall*.[13]
- Many of the mostly fair-skinned Celts had brown, red, or blonde hair. Male warriors let their hair and beards grow extra long for the "wild man" look. Women often fought alongside men.

- Celtic warriors wore thick gold rings called torcs around their necks. The men often fought naked.
- Celtic warriors often painted themselves blue (see "Why So Blue?") before battle. They also doused their hair with minerals, which made their long hair stand out in huge, scary spikes.
- They were fierce fighters and master horse handlers. They used long iron swords that could hack a man in two.
- Celts had a reputation for never giving up. Aristotle wrote that they were like men in a storm taunting lightning bolts.[14]
- Celtic warriors collected the decapitated heads of their enemies, drying them and then wearing them as trophies. Sometimes they hung the heads as decorations in their homes.

In between fighting, the Celts farmed the land and usually lived in circular homes with thatched roofs called roundhouses.

Celtic culture is all around us—if you know where to look. You'll find Celtic influence in jewelry and tattoo designs. Irish music and Scottish plaid have their roots in Celtic culture too. The Romans hadn't *kilt* everything.

### The Druids:
### From Female Furies to Fantasy Wizards

Was Boudicca a druid? It's hard to say. The Romans tell us she was a queen, a warrior, and a priestess, but not what *kind* of priestess. And, unfortunately, the only major accounts of druids come from the Romans (you know, the very people who *annihilated* the ancient religion), so it's hard to get an unbiased look at druid beliefs, rituals, and people.

Still, we can catch a glimpse of them in Roman descriptions of their attack on their sacred island during Boudicca's revolt.

Hardened Roman warriors froze with terror at first sight of the druids. Men and women stood defiant, a wall of people, many of them armed. Romans described the women among them as looking like "the Furies" (Greek and Roman goddesses of vengeance who were supposedly ugly, raging, winged creatures of the dark). They wore robes of "deathly black and with disheveled hair, they brandished their torches" while a circle of priests and priestesses raised their arms to the sky and invoked all kinds of deathly curses and evil upon their heads.[15]

Roman troops were shook.

It took a lot of yelling and threats to get them moving on the druids. Their general had to remind them "never to flinch before a band of females and fanatics." When they finally attacked, the Romans killed everyone and burned druid temples and sacred groves to the ground.

Still, the druids were not forgotten. Druidism has been romanticized in many fantasy epics, from Lord of the Rings to Harry Potter, where wise old men in druid-like robes carry secret, magical, or spiritual knowledge. Fighting male and female druids show up in popular online games such as World of Warcraft, as well as a wide variety of board and trading card games.

Fantasy writers, it seems, have often imagined druid priests as twinkly-eyed, cloak-wearing, white-bearded wizards. But as Dumbledore might say, alas, it's all fantasy, especially since these "wizards" were just as likely to be strong, fighting women as staff-carrying old men! Here's

what else we know about the religion from ancient sources:
- Celtic Druidism was a highly organized religion where women served alongside men as priests.
- It took twenty years of schooling to become a druid.
- Druids studied botany, mathematics, astronomy, and medicine. They were also masters of literature, poetry, and song.
- They passed on all their knowledge through storytelling (called the bardic tradition) rather than writing.
- They believed nature—the moon, sun, rain, and changing seasons—held mystical power. They considered mistletoe growing on oaks sacred.
- The Island of Mona (today's Anglesey, Wales) served as druid headquarters for Celtic tribes in and outside of Britain.
- Druids were so powerful that even tribal kings couldn't act without their advice. And if squabbling tribes began a war, druid priests could end it just by telling them to stop!
- They believed in reincarnation—that the soul passed on to live new lives.
- They practiced ritual human sacrifice, which often occurred around the seasons. For example, some took place in the autumn around the time of the Celtic festival known as Samhain—today's Halloween. (You wouldn't want to go trick-or-treating around their neighborhood, that's for sure.)

Some people like to imagine that the druids had special mystical powers. And maybe they did—who knows? They certainly had staying power. Despite Rome's attempts at extinguishing them, the druids live on in our imaginations through enduring fantasy stories and legends.

### Why So Blue?

The ancient Celts often painted themselves blue before battle. Why? Nobody knows for sure, but the Celts may have believed the color provided mystical protection. And it turns out they may have been partly right. Scientists have found that the plant the Celts used for bluing-up—woad—has antiseptic properties. In other words, it may have helped prevent infections from sword cuts.

Woad, a native British plant related to the broccoli plant, produces blue dye. Spread over the body, woad dye also has psychotropic properties—which means it can cause a dreamlike state.[16] Some think Celtic warriors used woad to make themselves "crazy fierce" before battle.

Turns out the Celts and the druids knew a bit more than we thought about "biological" warfare. They may, in fact, have been *true-blue* geniuses!

### Boudicca, Druids, and Human Sacrifice

Around thirty-five years ago, a couple of guys cutting up chunks of thick, grassy mud (peat) in Cheshire, England, stumbled upon a body. So they called the police.

*Yup, it looked like murder*, the officers said. They began investigating. Had anyone gone missing recently? Anybody see anything suspicious?

Back at the lab, doctors discovered something shocking: the body of Lindow Man—as he was called because he was found in the Lindow Moss bog—was actually a 2,000-year-old Celt.[17] The bog had preserved the body so well that investigators thought he'd been recently murdered.

Imagine their shock when they carbon-dated the evidence and discovered it dated to about the time of Boudicca's rebellion!

Was Lindow Man sacrificed to the Celtic gods in a desperate attempt to keep the Romans off their back during Boudicca's war? Some archaeologists think so. Why? Because his death had all the markings of a ritual.

First, Lindow Man was clubbed on the head three times. Some think he may have been kneeling at the time. Then he was strangled with a rope that had three knots at the back. And then, just for good measure, his throat was cut.

The number three often had spiritual meaning, and Lindow Man got hurt in triplicate. He had three blows to the head, three knots in the rope, and three types of attacks.

Three was definitely *not* the charm for the poor victim!

Scientists have discovered that Lindow Man was in his midtwenties. His beard had been trimmed. His fingernails were clean. That's why some think he was a druid priest. After all, he didn't have the battle scars of a warrior or the dirty nails of a farmer. Doctors also found mistletoe pollen in his stomach, suggesting that the ritual took place in a sacred grove. Druid priests believed mistletoe was holy.

Lindow Man may have even volunteered to be sacrificed. The Romans were destroying their people, lands, and religion. Maybe sacrificing a priest would end their misery. But in the end, it didn't. One murder in the woods did nothing to stop the killing in the fields.

## CHAPTER NOTES

[1] — Suetonius claimed that Caesar originally invaded Britain "with the hope of getting pearls" and that he was an "enthusiastic collector of gems."

[2] — Suetonius points out that Claudius selected Britain *because* no one had tried since Julius Caesar and it was likely the easiest target for a military success.

The British are so proud of their ancient Celtic queen, they placed a bronze statue of her near the House of Parliament and Westminster Abbey.

[3] — Tacitus tells us that Boudicca's husband wrote his will in such a way that would "place his kingdom and household beyond the risk of injury." It did the opposite.

[4] — Strabo claims that all Celts were "war-mad and both high-spirited and quick for battle." This was true for the Iceni as well. Taking away their weapons was an insult to their heroic identity.

[5]— While Celtic society was definitely a "man's world," women were highly respected: "A Celtic woman had rights and powers that even Cleopatra might have envied," wrote historian Philip Freeman.

[6]— The Romans were terrified of druidism, declaring that it contained "monstrous rites."

[7]— Tacitus wrote that the Roman thug who started the whole thing, Catus Decianus, sailed away to Gaul.

[8]— Proof of Boudicca's revolt—as well as countless other major events—is still being discovered during digs for trains and/or buildings.

[9]— Rome claimed Boudicca led an unruly mob of savages, but she was the first to unite the tribes of Britain. Plus, she got within a cat's whisker of pushing Rome off the island altogether.

[10]—Cassius Dio also wrote that she took a hare out of her robe and let it run free, which the Britons saw as an "auspicious" sign. They would get their freedom. But the only freedom most of them got was death.

[11]—Great legends have grown regarding where Boudicca's body might be found. The silliest one? She lies buried beneath Platform 10 at King's Cross Station in London.

[12]—Julius Caesar wrote about the druids in his famous book about his conquest of the Celts in France and Germany.

[13]—The Celts likely teased Alexander the Great about his height because he was on the short side. Strabo says that right after that jibe, though, they tried to make up for it by claiming that his friendship was "above all else." Nice save, Celts!

[14]—Aristotle claimed that the Celts' fearlessness and bravery bordered on "madness" and that they dipped their newborns in freezing rivers to toughen them up.

[15]—Tacitus described druid women as looking like Furies. Roman soldiers, he claimed, were frozen with fear at the sight of them.

[16]—The mind-altering consequences of woad, however, may have only lasted two hours—just enough time for battle!

[17]—Carbon dating on Lindow Man narrowed the date of his life to sometime in the first century. A number of archaeologists believe his sacrifice was related to Boudicca's revolt.

Was Lindow Man sacrificed during Boudicca's revolt? Some archaeologists say it's possible.

# CHAPTER SIX

# ZENOBIA

## ZEALOUSLY ZAPPING HER ENEMIES

Two hundred years after Boudicca, another brilliant queen named Zenobia also tried to kick the Romans to the curb. And thanks to a fast female camel, she almost succeeded. Unfortunately, a giant hump got in her way.

It all started in 270 CE when Zenobia was the queen of Palmyra, the beautiful oasis known as the City of Palms in today's Syria. Palmyra stood between two empires—Rome on one side and Persia (Iraq/Iran) on the other. Poor Palmyra was the only buffer between them. Palmyrans must have felt like the last lemon tree near a lemonade stand. It was only a matter of time before somebody squeezed them dry.

But Palmyra made its position work by becoming a key

trading post. Almost all Eastern goods flowed through the city into Rome.

The problems started with the assassination of Zenobia's hubby, the king.[1] Some figured Rome was behind the murder, even though Palmyra was a Roman province, which meant the Palmyran king reported to the Roman emperor. So why would the Romans kill one of their "own"?

Most likely because he wielded a little too much power in the region. Rome never quite trusted the kings and queens in their Eastern empire. They worried that one powerful leader could incite rebellion against them. And that Zenobia's husband was the kind of leader who would do just that. So they took him out.

Only one problem.

He wasn't the one they should've been worrying about. The queen was much more dangerous.

And even when that queen marched an army into other Roman-held territories, they still couldn't believe it.

## "You're Kidding, Right?"

A woman on the attack? Rome didn't take her seriously at first. (Would they never learn?) After all, she was a mere woman. But they must have forgotten that the region had a long history of tough-as-desert-grit queens. She was following in the tradition of famous warrior queens such as Queen Zabibi and Queen Samsi,

who ruled nearly 1,000 years before Zenobia, not to mention Syrian queens before her, such as Tryphaena, Berenice, and the infamous Egyptian queen, Cleopatra VII.

Taking a page out of her own regional history book, Zenobia went on the attack. Her goal: to take Roman-controlled territories and rule over them. Why, she must have figured, should all their wealth and resources go to prop up a foreign overlord that barely showed them respect?

So Zenobia went on a campaign to convince her neighbors to rebel with her. Her timing was good. Many locals were tired of dealing with the Western superpower.[2] They liked the idea of local control. Those whom she couldn't persuade with words she convinced by the sword.

She sparked the flames of rebellion like a pyromaniac with a brand-new box of matches.

It helped that Rome looked like it was teetering on the brink of collapse. Persian enemies had recently defeated a Roman general, and his replacement was busy with German invaders attacking Rome's northern territories.

It was the perfect time to hold Rome's feet to the fire.[3]

## While the Cat's Away, the Mice Will . . . Tear It Up!

Zenobia led her army into parts of Jordan and Judea (ancient Israel) first. Then she took over Egypt. Smart move. After all, Rome depended on Egypt for its grain. Nothing like the threat of starvation to make someone pay attention, right?

Zenobia modeled herself as the new Cleopatra. Cleopatra VII was an Egyptian queen who had fought Rome for independent control of Egypt 300 years earlier. (Too bad the queen forgot one little detail: Cleopatra *lost*.) Zenobia even claimed Cleopatra was a distant ancestor—which wasn't as far-fetched as it sounded. Many believed Cleopatra was part Syrian. And, like Cleopatra, Zenobia spoke multiple languages, including Egyptian.

Still, not all Egyptians were happy about Zenobia taking over, long-lost family connection or not. They weren't so sure about trading one master for another. And if she didn't succeed, they didn't want to face Rome's wrath.

After all, Rome's territorial philosophy could be boiled down to a single simple idea: violence is *always* the answer.

Why provoke them?

But one look at Zenobia's forces and skeptics were convinced. By the time she was done marauding through the region, Zenobia had taken Syria, Judea, Egypt, and a large part of Asia Minor (today's Turkey) from the Romans.

To say the Romans were caught off guard is like saying the Grand Canyon is a small hole in the ground.

## Beware the Tantrums of a Man Bested by a Woman!

Because Zenobia's region had long histories of strong queens in charge, she may not have anticipated just how angry and shamed Aurelian, the emperor-general of Rome, would feel about her attacks. After all, Rome had never had a woman in power. And, like the ancient Greeks, Romans believed women should have few rights. To lose territories to a queen was shameful.

Aurelian's enemies pounced on his losses to weaken his hold on power. But he wasn't fighting just the queen, he complained. Zenobia commanded a "great force of the enemy"![4]

While Zenobia was busy uniting the region under her control, the emperor of Rome dropped his border battles in Germania and marched huge armies back into the Middle East. He snatched Egypt back first, as well as other key cities.

To give you an idea of the type of opponent Zenobia faced, the Romans recorded this story about their emperor-general: Aurelian had a royal meltdown when the citizens of Tyana refused to open their gates to him. The insult of people choosing loyalty to a *queen* over him was just too much. He was madder than a cut snake.

If Tyana didn't let him in immediately, "I will not leave even a dog alive!" he roared in an epic temper tantrum.[5]

The townspeople, marking the size of his army—and how far away Zenobia's forces were—reluctantly opened their gates and surrendered. They likely hoped their quick about-face would keep the hot-tempered emperor from punishing them too harshly. The emperor's soldiers had other ideas: like thirsty vampires breaking in to party at the blood bank, they demanded the right to go on a killing and plundering spree.

But Aurelian knew destroying the entire city would not play well against Zenobia's call for freedom from Roman oppression. The emperor had to think fast. To prove that he was a man of his word, he gave an alternate order: *Kill all the dogs!*

He'd said he would not leave "even a dog alive" in the city, hadn't he? Sadly for the dogs, being as good as his word was not at all good for them. His soldiers *slaughtered every dog in the city!* Poor pooches—sacrificed in the name of one man's ego.

What did Zenobia make of all this? We don't know, but we can guess she wanted to throw Aurelian headfirst into the doghouse.

## The Battle Begins

While Aurelian was trying to prove he was top dog by killing innocent pups, the queen and her growing forces continued to rampage. Aurelian caught up with Zenobia's army outside the Syrian city of Antioch. The queen galloped on horseback up and down the line, inspiring her warriors as they prepared for battle.

The time was right to kick Rome out of their backyard once and for all, she reminded them.

Aurelian took one look at the size of her army and must've figured he couldn't win outright, so he planned a trick. As the armies faced off, he gave the order: "Retreat!" His men began running for their lives. Zenobia's army followed, thinking they'd whupped the Romans good. But her soldiers didn't notice that this "retreat" sure seemed pretty orderly.

One more thing: The Romans were lightly armed and armored. The Palmyrians, on the other hand, wore full, heavy armor. And as they chased the Romans through the desert, they began to broil in their own personal Easy-Bake™ ovens. That's when Romans turned and attacked.

Overheated, tired, and trapped, Zenobia's forces fell hard as Romans quickly began doing what they did best: cutting everyone down. They weren't considered the killing machine of the ancient world for nothing.

Somehow, Zenobia and her most loyal generals escaped the massacre and returned to Antioch. The queen kept the city on her side with a trick of her own. Her general captured a Roman that looked like Aurelian and marched the chained body double through the city, pretending that they had defeated the Romans.[6] This gave Zenobia the ability to round up enough fighters to take on the real Aurelian when he returned.

And return he did, demolishing her remaining forces outside the city of Emesa. It looked like the end for Zenobia. But this fierce queen wasn't ready to give up yet.

She took off to Palmyra, hoping for backup from the fellow Rome-haters with whom she shared a border: the Persians.

Unfortunately for her, the Persians weren't prepared for a

full-out war with their old nemesis; they turned their backs on her. She was on her own.

## "Surrender Now!"

As Aurelian chased her, he got angrier and angrier. His soldiers continually faced harassment from her army. He wanted her to call the whole thing off, so he sent Zenobia a letter, hoping a promise to spare her life would do the trick.[7]

The queen zinged him back with this: "You demand my surrender as though you were not aware that Cleopatra preferred to die a queen rather than remain alive." Then she announced that she had reinforcements from Persia—Rome's bitter enemy—on their way to help her. Which wasn't true, but she wasn't about to tell *him* that.

Aurelian was furious. "How, O Zenobia," he ranted, "have you dared to insult Roman emperors!"

But insult him she did. Especially when she added that she wanted to share power, to "become a partner," and rule the East with Rome.[8]

A woman as an equal partner?

Queen, please.

Romans would sooner see their empire crumble into a black pit of misery, death, and destruction than share power with a woman. Oh wait, that is *exactly* what happened in the Middle Ages. But still.

## "A Camel! A Camel! My Kingdom for a Camel!"

Zenobia hightailed it back to her home city of Palmyra. The Romans followed in hot pursuit. The key word being "hot." The Syrian deserts were excruciating. But the Romans made it in time to trap Zenobia inside the city walls. They would starve her and her supporters out if needed, plus keep out any Persian reinforcements that tried to help.

Zenobia must have realized her cause was doomed. Her only hope was escaping to Persia and convincing her neighbors to renew warfare with their mutual enemy.

After all, if the queen was anything, it was *persuasive*. Zenobia could've sold sand to a scorpion.

So she snuck out of her city riding a female camel. Female camels, supposedly, were even faster than horses. But her plans were foiled. Someone betrayed her to the Romans. They caught up with her, dragged her away, and sacked Palmyra.

The tenacious queen, meanwhile, would finally come face-to-face with the furious emperor of Rome.

## "What Will My Friends Think?"

If Zenobia had been a man, Aurelian would've probably killed her on the spot as payback for all the aggravation she'd caused him, but he likely worried about his image back home. After all, he didn't want to go down in history as the guy who cut the throat of a woman, enemy or not.

Zenobia, for her part, blamed her male advisors for the uprising. Talk about passing the buck! But who knows, maybe her plan was to have her advisors punished so that she could be free to continue the resistance when the focus was off her.

Either way, Aurelian spared her life so that he could drag her in chains in his victory parades. And parade her he did. He marched her in heavy golden chains through every Middle Eastern city on the way back to Rome. The message was clear: don't even *think* about rebelling like Zenobia.

Perhaps the queen stood too tall and with too much dignity for his taste because by the time they got to Rome's victory parade, Aurelian weighed her down so heavily in chains that she needed help to stand upright.[9]

Marching before Zenobia came a group of Goth women, female warriors from ancient Germany who had been captured fighting in men's clothes. Aurelian had a sign around their necks claiming they were Amazons.

(The ancient Greeks believed true heroes always tussled with Amazon warriors and won, if you recall from Artemisia's story on page 52. This was Aurelian's way of propping himself up as a hero in the old tradition.)

As for Zenobia, she pulled up the rear. And when it was all over, Aurelian did the unexpected: he gave her a villa to live in. Later, she married a Roman senator and lived the life of a "good Roman wife."

No single act could've been more helpful to Rome. After

all, her followers might have continued fighting if she'd been martyred. But they quickly forgot all about her when she became a Roman housewife.

Too bad we don't have a clue what Zenobia thought about how her life ended up. For all we know, she continued planning a rebellion from Rome. She certainly seemed stubborn enough to try.

Or maybe, like a soldier in the mess hall, she'd just finally had her fill.

## A Zesty Visionary

Still, history remembers Zenobia as the brave warrior queen who almost toppled the Roman Empire in the East. And the funny thing is, like Cleopatra before her, she anticipated what happened anyway.

Both queens tried to convince Rome that the best way to manage its enormous empire was to have a strong ruler in the eastern territories work *with* Rome, as its partner. But Rome refused to consider the option, especially since it meant sharing power with a woman.

They should've listened. Sixty years after Zenobia, in 330 CE, Emperor Constantine moved his capital to Byzantium in today's Turkey, setting up the split that would eventually end with the fall of Rome in the West.

Had Rome kept that region stable via partnering with strong queens like Zenobia, perhaps they wouldn't have stretched themselves and the empire to the breaking point. In the end, moving the center of the Roman world to Byzantium weakened the West, leaving Rome vulnerable to invading hordes. It wasn't long after that the West largely fell into illiteracy and infighting during the Middle Ages, while the East thrived both creatively and intellectually.

What would've happened if Aurelian—and the Roman leader during the war with Cleopatra before him—had agreed to share power with a queen of the East? Would they have created a world where men and women shared power more equally, a world where West and East cooperated for mutual benefit rather than—as ended up happening—battling for individual dominance?

We'll never know. But we can thank the strong women of the ancient world who lost their lives in pursuit of that dream.

Without them, history wouldn't be half as interesting.

### Show Me the Money

Did Zenobia really intend to kick Rome out of the region? Or was she just trying to consolidate her family's power? The answer could be in the money.[10] Some coins of the era show Zenobia's son (he would succeed her on the throne), Vaballathus, on one side and Aurelian on the other. The emperor's image on the coin implies loyalty to Rome. But other coins minted during the rebellion show her queenly profile on one side and the goddess Juno (Roman queen of the gods) on the other, no emperor in sight! Was this an evolution of ambition on her part? Did she think it was time for the queen of the region and the queen of Olympus to rule over the land? Whatever her ultimate goal, the queen certainly used both sides of her coin to demand change.

### Palmyra in the News

Zenobia's city, Palmyra, northeast of today's Damascus in Syria, has been a treasure trove for archaeologists for centuries. They have uncovered the remnants of the queen's palace, the marketplace, and even the marble theater where she likely caught a show or two.

Unfortunately, war in the region has left the digs in ruins.

Palmyra has been under attack for years by the Islamic State, a group of extremists who want to make strict religious rule the law of the land in Iraq and Syria.

Even though the city is a protected world heritage UNESCO site, it hasn't stopped insurgents from attacking. Archaeologists weep over the damage done to irreplaceable antiquities. Thankfully, the city was reclaimed from violent extremists in early 2017.[11] Unfortunately, the Islamic State returned, and fighting is still ongoing at press time (2019). A worldwide effort is underway to protect the priceless ruins, but there's no guarantee of success.

### The Roman Fear of Strong, Powerful Women

The Romans had a long history of being uncomfortable with strong, ambitious, independent women, especially "foreign" women from the East. Their stories and myths are filled with beautiful, wealthy, powerful women who almost took down otherwise "good and virtuous" men.

132

The idea of women who wouldn't be controlled or fit into the narrow boxes of acceptable behavior scared them. They called such women troublemakers. Since a great deal of Roman culture comes from the ancient Greeks—who did not respect women—it is no surprise that the Romans used Greek myths to reinforce their fears. Stories of treacherous women were a popular theme:

- Helen of Troy caused a great war to break out because of her dangerous beauty.
- Amazon warriors *dared* to combat Hercules, Achilles, Theseus, and other Greek and Roman heroes (and always had to be either defeated or die in the telling).[12]
- The war against Egypt and Cleopatra was largely fueled by hatred and fear of the "evil" queen who dared partner with one of Rome's top generals in an effort to "unman" the Romans.[13]
- Dido of Carthage almost kept Aeneas from fulfilling his duty of founding Rome.

Roman anxiety over strong women guaranteed that they would fight to the bitter end to stop those "horrible foreign queens" from taking more power or wealth than they thought they should have.

Zenobia openly identified herself with Cleopatra, the last pharaoh of Egypt. Queen Cleopatra and her consort, the Roman general Marc Antony, fought a war with Rome for control and power. Although she ended up losing, Cleopatra's wealth and power made a lasting impression on the Romans. They never quite got over their fear of her, which was why Zenobia claimed connection to the ancient queen. And given the way she almost snatched victory from the relentless Romans, she wasn't that *pharaoh-off*, was she?

133

# CHAPTER NOTES

[1] — Rumor had it that the Roman emperor had the Palmyran king/Zenobia's husband, Odaenathus, killed, which may explain her aggressive attack.

[2] — Zenobia created a Palmyran stronghold in these regions while acting as regent for her son. Her wisdom lay in her ability to win the allegiance of the disenfranchised in both Egypt and Syria.

Queen Zenobia (depicted here as the goddess Ishtar) wanted to free the region from Roman control and rule in their place.

[3] — Archaeologist and Zenobia expert Judith Weingarten agrees on Zenobia's smart timing: "Romans could no longer defend the East." Plus, she adds, "Rome was corrupt."

[4]— The source for this "The Life of Aurelian" letter from the *Historia Augusta* by Flavian Vopiscus is not considered by scholars as very "reliable," but it is all we have on the queen given that "there are no contemporary historical texts."

[5]— The dog story takes place in Tyana. The killing of all the dogs—rather than the people of the city—was seen by the Romans as a noble act.

[6]— Zenobia's pretense of victory was a display of "pure theater" to buy time for her and her forces to regroup.

[7]— Aurelian promised to "spare their lives" if they gave up. He also demanded that Zenobia hand over all her treasure in exchange for not killing all the people of Palmyra.

[8]— Zenobia, according to Zosimus, a Byzantine historian, claimed that she asked to become "a partner in the royal power, should the supply of lands permit." Rome never even considered it.

[9]— Aurelian also paraded exotic animals—such as elephants—from conquered lands. These he gave to prominent Romans for their gardens—a nifty way to avoid the cost of feeding the beasts.

Minting her own coins and replacing the image of the Roman emperor with her own was Zenobia's declaration of war.

[10]—Author Antonia Fraser claimed that when Zenobia minted her own coins, it served as a signal of rebellion, a kind of declaration of war against Rome.

[11]—The Associated Press reported March 2, 2017, that the Syrian army retook Palmyra from the occupying extremists only to find a great deal of destruction. Archaeologists are working around the clock to preserve what they can.

[12]—Adrienne Mayor's *The Amazons* gives an outstanding overview of the way Amazons were depicted in myth and legend in the ancient world.

[13]—Cleopatra became the scapegoat for Octavian's war against Marc Antony. It was actually a civil war between two Roman leaders, but Octavian (later known as Caesar Augustus) convinced Romans that the "evil" queen of Egypt had to be stopped.

# EPILOGUE

## Never Underestimate the Power of a Strong Woman with a Plan

As the old saying goes, well-behaved women rarely make history. Lucky for us and for their people, the ancient queens in this book weren't interested in behaving in any kind of way that diminished their power.

And they were not alone.

Women have stood up to fight for their families, territories, and nations in every corner of the world from the dawn of time.

In modern times, women have ruled as presidents or prime ministers in Germany, Britain, Poland, Taiwan, Chile, Myanmar, New Zealand, and many other countries. Women lead as military commanders and generals around the world too. They stand on the shoulders of all the powerful queens, warriors, and rulers throughout history whose stories were either ignored or erased.

The fearless, kick-butt women of today are making the history of tomorrow. Only this time, thankfully, their stories will be recorded in detail for future generations.

And, we can imagine, like the warrior queens of old, they're encouraging us to go *forth and slay*—in our own ways.

# ENDNOTES

## Chapter One

[1]—page 14. W. V. Davies, "Egypt and Nubia," eds. Dreyfus, Keller and Roehrig, *Hatshepsut: From Queen to Pharaoh*, (New Haven, Yale University Press, 2005), page 51.

[2]—page 15. Kara Cooney, *The Woman Who Would Be King*, (New York, Crown, 2014), page 53.

[3]—page 15. Cooney, page 40.

[4]—page 16. Cooney, page 64.

[5]—page 17. C. A. Keller, "The Joint Reign of Hatshepsut and Thutmose III." *Hatshepsut: From Queen to Pharaoh*, page 96.

[6]—page 17. Davies, *Hatshepsut: From Queen to Pharaoh*, page 53.

[7]—page 18. Elizabeth Carney, "Women and Military Leadership in Pharaonic Egypt," *Greek, Roman, and Byzantine Studies*, page 33. Also, "Hatshepsut and the Tomb Beneath the Tomb," Judith Weingarten, Zenobia: Empress of the East blog, March 15, 2009. http://judithweingarten.blogspot.com/2009/03/hatshepsut-and-tomb-beneath-tomb.html.

[8]—page 18. Frederick Monderson, *Hatshepsut's Temple at Deir el-Bahari*, (Brooklyn, CreateSpace, 2011), page 42.

[9]—page 18. Anthony J. Spalinger, *War in Ancient Egypt: The New Kingdom* (Hoboken, John Wiley & Sons, 2008), page 132.

[10]—page 20. Gay Robins, *Women in Ancient Egypt*, (Cambridge, Harvard University Press, 1993), page 46.

[11]—page 21. Robins, page 21.

[12]—page 22. Elizabeth B. Wilson, "The Woman Who Would Be King." *Smithsonian*, September, 2006. https://www.smithsonianmag.com/issue/september-2006/.

*Websites active at time of publication*

[13]—page 23. A. M. Roth, "Models of Authority." *Hatshepsut: From Queen to Pharaoh*, page 10.

[14]—page 23. Joyce Tyldesly, *Hatshepsut*, (London, Penguin Books, 1996), page 225.

[15]—page 25. A. M. Roth, "Erasing a Reign." *Hatshepsut: From Queen to Pharaoh*, page 281.

[16]—page 26. Zahi Hawass, "The Scientific Search for Hatshepsut's Mummy." *KMT: A Modern Journal of Ancient Egypt*. Volume 18, Number 3, Fall 2007, pages 20–25.

## Chapter Two

[1]—page 33. Polyaenus, *Stratagems of War*, Book 8, section 53. http://www.attalus.org/translate/polyaenus8B.html.

[2]—page 36. Vesta S. Curtis and Sarah Stewart, *The Birth of the Persian Empire: The Idea of Iran*, (London, I.B. Tauris, 2005), page 5.

[3]—page 36. Barry Strauss, *The Battle of Salamis: The Naval Encounter That Saved Greece—and Western Civilization*, (New York, Simon and Schuster, 2004), page 37.

[4]—page 37. Jona Lendering, "Earth and Water," 1997. http://www.livius.org/articles/concept/earth-and-water.

[5]—page 38. Strauss, *The Battle of Salamis*, page 34.

[6]—page 38. Strauss, page 33.

[7]—page 38. Herodotus, *The Histories*, 7.224. http://www.perseus.tufts.edu/hopper/text?doc=Perseus%3 Atext%3A1999.01.0126%3Abook%3D7%3Achapter%3D224.

[8]—page 39. John R. Hale, *Lords of the Sea: The Epic Story of the Athenian Navy and the Birth of Democracy*, (New York, Viking, 2009), page 33. Also, *Herodotus, The Histories*, 7.99. http://www.perseus.tufts.edu/hopper/text?doc=Perseus:abo:tlg,0016,001:7:99.

[9]—page 39. Strauss, *The Battle of Salamis*, page 98.

[10]—page 40. Strauss, page 41.

[11]—page 41. Herodotus, *The Histories*, 8.69. http://www.perseus.tufts.edu/hopper/text?doc=Perseus:abo:tlg,0016,001:8.

[12]—page 44. Strauss, *The Battle of Salamis*, page 188.

[13]—page 44. Herodotus, *The Histories*, 7.99.1. http://www.perseus.tufts.edu/hopper/text?doc=Perseus%3Atext%3A1999.01.0126%3Abook%3D7%3Achapter%3D99%3Asection%3D1.

[14]—page 45. Herodotus, *The Histories*, 8.104. http://www.perseus.tufts.edu/hopper/text?doc=Perseus:abo:tlg,0016,001:8.

[15]—page 52. Adrienne Mayor, *The Amazons: Lives and Legends of Warrior Women across the Ancient World*, (Princeton, Princeton University Press, 2014), page 314.

[16]—page 53. Mayor, pages 63–64.

[17]—page 53. Mayor, page 413.

[18]—page 54. Paul Woodruff, *First Democracy: The Challenge of an Ancient Idea*, (New York, Oxford University Press, 2005), page 36.

## Chapter Three

[1]—page 60. Robert G. Morkot, *The Black Pharaohs: Egypt's Nubian Rulers*, (London, Rubicon Press, 2000), page 1.

[2]—page 61. Robert Steven Bianchi, *Daily Life of the Nubians*, (Westport, Greenwood Press, 2004), page 217.

[3]—page 64. Toyin Falola, *Key Events in African History: A Reference Guide*, (Westport, Greenwood Press, 2002), page 56.

[4]—page 64. Adrian Goldsworthy, *Augustus: First Emperor of Rome*, (New Haven, Yale University Press, 2014), page 206.

[5]—page 65. Strabo, Book 17.1.54. http://www.perseus.tufts.edu/hopper/text?doc=Perseus%3Atext%3A1999.01.0239%3Abook%3D17%3Achapter%3D1%3Asection%3D54.

[6]—page 66. Strabo, Book 17.1.54. http://www.perseus.tufts.edu/hopper/text?doc=Perseus%3Atext%3A1999.01.0239%3Abook%3D17%3Achapter%3D1%3Asection%3D54.

[7]—page 67. Strabo, Book 17.1.54. http://www.perseus.tufts.edu/hopper/text?doc=Perseus%3Atext%3A1999.01.0239%3Abook%3D17%3Achapter%3D1%3Asection%3D54.

[8]—page 68. Strabo, Book 17.1.54. http://www.perseus.tufts.edu/hopper/text?doc=Perseus%3Atext%3A1999.01.0239%3Abook%3D17%3Achapter%3D1%3Asection%3D54.

[9]—page 69. UNESCO.com, "World Heritage Committee inscribes five new sites in Colombia, Sudan, Jordan, Italy and Germany."

[10]—page 70. "Gold and the Gods: Jewels of Ancient Nubia:" July 2014–January 2017. Museum of Fine Arts, Boston: http://www.mfa.org/exhibitions/gold-and-gods.

[11]—page 70. Morkot, *The Black Pharaohs: Egypt's Nubian Rulers*, page 2.

[12]—page 71. Haynes and Santini-Ritt, "Women in Ancient Nubia," (eds. M. Fisher, P. Lacovara, et al), *Ancient Nubia: African Kingdoms of the Nile*, (Cairo, American University in Cairo Press, 2012), page 183.

[13]—page 72. Falola, *Key Events in African History: A Reference Guide*, page 57.

[14]—page 72. Karen Workman, "When You're Named Isis for the Goddess, Not the Terror Group," *New York Times*, November, 2015.

[15]—page 73. G. Armelagos, K. Kolbacher, K. Collins, J. Cook, M. Krafeld-Daughtery, "Tetracycline Consumption in Prehistory." *Tetracyclines in Biology, Chemistry and Medicine*, eds, M. Nelson, W. Hillen, R.A. Greenwald, (Basel, Switzerland, Springer Basel AG, 2001), page 223.

## Chapter Four

[1]—page 78. M. Vo and Nguyen Ngoc Bich, *The Trung Sisters Revisited*, (Lexington, CreateSpace, 2015), page 24.

[2]—page 79. William Stewart Logan, *Hanoi: Biography of a City*, (Seattle, University of Washington Press, 2000), page 45.

[3]—page 79. John P. McKay, et al., *Understanding World Societies, Volume I*, (Bedford, St. Martins, second edition, 2015), page 134.

[4]—page 82. Vo and Bich, *The Trung Sisters Revisited*, page 29.

[5]—page 83. Keith Weller Taylor, *The Birth of Vietnam*, (Berkeley, University of California Press, 1991), page 77.

[6]—page 84. Vo and Bich, *The Trung Sisters Revisited*, page 34.

[7]—page 86. Vo and Bich, *The Trung Sisters Revisited*, page 38.

[8]—page 86. Marc Jason Gilbert, "When Heroism is Not Enough: Three Women Warriors of Vietnam, Their Historians and World History," *World History Connected*, 2007, http://worldhistoryconnected.press. uillinois.edu/4.3/gilbert.html.

[9]—page 87. Stanley Sandler, *Ground Warfare: An International Encyclopedia, Volume 1*, (Santa Barbara, ABC-CLIO, 2002), page 43.

[10]—page 88. Sud Chonchirdsin, "Why a Proverb Calls the Vietnamese the 'Children of the Dragon and the Grandchildren of the Fairy.'" https://scroll.in/article/830807/why-the-vietnamese-are-called-the-children-of-the-dragon-and-grandchildren-of-the-fairy.

[11]—page 89. Gilbert, "When Heroism is Not Enough: Three Women Warriors of Vietnam, Their Historians and World History," *World History Connected*.

[12]—page 90. Douglas A. Phillips, *Vietnam*, (New York, Chelsea House, 2006), page 31.

[13]—page 90. Taylor, *The Birth of Vietnam*, page 90.

## Chapter Five

[1]—page 95. Suetonius, "Caesar," *Lives of the Caesars*, 47.1 http:// penelope.uchicago.edu/Thayer/E/Roman/Texts/Suetonius/12Caesars/ Julius*.html.

[2]—page 98. Suetonius, 17.2. http://penelope.uchicago.edu/Thayer/e/ roman/texts/suetonius/12caesars/claudius.html.

[3]—page 99. Tacitus, *Annals*, Book XIV, 31.1. http://penelope.uchicago. edu/Thayer/E/Roman/Texts/Tacitus/Annals/14B.html.

[4]—page 99. Strabo, Book IX, Chapter 4.2. http://penelope.uchicago.
edu/Thayer/e/roman/texts/strabo/4d.html.

[5]—page 100. Philip Freeman, *The Philosopher and the Druids: A Journey Among the Ancient Celts*, (New York, Simon and Schuster, 2006), page 4.

[6]—page 101. Pliny the Elder, *The Natural Histories*, Book 30.4. Perseus Digital Library. http://www.perseus.tufts.edu/hopper/text?doc= Perseus%3Atext%3A1999.02.0137%3Abook%3D30%3A chapter%3D4.

[7]—page 102. Tacitus, *Annals*, 14.32. http://penelope.uchicago.edu/Thayer/E/Roman/Texts/Tacitus/Annals/14B.html.

[8]—page 104. Roff Smith, "London's Big Dig Reveals Amazing Layers of History," *National Geographic*, February 2016. http://ngm.nationalgeographic.com/2016/02/artifacts-found-under-london-archaeology-text.

[9]—page 104. Philip Matyszak, *The Enemies of Rome: From Hannibal to Attila the Hun*, (Thames and Hudson, London, 2009), page 185. Also, M.J. Trow, *Boudicca: The Warrior Queen*, (Gloucestershire, Sutton Publishing, 2003), page 136.

[10]—page 106. Cassius Dio, *Roman History*, Book 62.6. http://penelope.uchicago.edu/Thayer/e/roman/texts/cassius_dio/62.html.

[11]—page 107. Trow, page 198.

[12]—page 109. Caesar, *The Gallic Wars*, Book VI.XIII.

[13]—page 109. Strabo, *Geography*, 7.3.8. http://www.perseus.tufts.edu/hopper/text?doc=Perseus%3Atext%3A1999.01.0198%3 Abook%3D7%3Achapter%3D3%3Asection%3D8.

[14]—page 110. Freeman, *Philosopher and the Druids*, page 28. Also, Vicky Alvear Shecter, *Alexander the Great Rocks the World*, page 33.

[15]—page 111. Tacitus, *Annals*, 14.37.1. http://penelope.uchicago.edu/Thayer/E/Roman/Texts/Tacitus/Annals/14B.html.

[16]—page 113. David W. Group, *Encyclopedia of Mind Enhancing Foods, Drugs and Nutritional Substances*, (Jefferson, McFarland and Company, Inc., 2015), page 261.

[17]—page 113. Trow, pages 85–88.

## Chapter Six

[1]—page 119. Alaric Watson, *Aurelian and the Third Century*, (London, Routledge, 1999), page 56.

[2]—page 122. Prudence Jones, "Rewriting Power: Zenobia, Aurelian, and the Historia Augusta," *Classical World*, vol. 109, no. 2, (Johns Hopkins University Press, Winter 2016), page 222.

 [3]—page 122. Judith Weingarten, "Why Did She Do It?" *Zenobia: Empress of the East*. http://judithweingarten.blogspot.com/2007/01/why-did-she-do-it.html.

[4]—page 124. Judith Weingarten, "Now All Shame is Exhausted . . ." *Zenobia: Empress of the East*. http://judithweingarten.blogspot.com/2008/06/now-all-shame-is-exhausted.html.

 [5]—page 124. Vopiscus, *Historia Augusta*, 23.2. http://penelope.uchicago.edu/Thayer/E/Roman/Texts/Historia_Augusta/Aurelian/2.html#37.

[6]—page 126. Mitch Williamson, "Zenobia and Aurelian's March to Syria," *Weapons and Warfare: History and Hardware of Warfare*, July 13, 2017. https://weaponsandwarfare.com/2017/07/13/zenobia-and-aurelians-march-to-syria/.

[7]—page 127. Vopiscus, *Historia Augusta*, 26.7. http://penelope.uchicago.edu/Thayer/E/Roman/Texts/Historia_Augusta/Aurelian/2.html#26.7.

[8]—page 127. Antonia Fraser, *The Warrior Queens: The Legends and Lives of the Women Who Have Led Their Nations in War*, (New York, Anchor, 1990), page 123.

[9]—page 129. Vopicus, 33.5. http://penelope.uchicago.edu/Thayer/E/Roman/Texts/Historia_Augusta/Aurelian/2.html#33.

[10]—page 131. Fraser, *The Warrior Queens: The Legends and Lives of the Women Who Have Led Their Nations in War,* page 119.

[11]—page 132. Philip Issa, "Syrian Army Re-Enters Town of Palmyra as IS Defenses Crumbles," March 2, 2017.

[12]—page 133. Adrienne Mayor, *The Amazons: Lives and Legends of Warrior Women across the Ancient World,* (Princeton, Princeton University Press, 2014).

[13]—page 133. Vicky Alvear Shecter, *Cleopatra Rules: The Amazing Life of the Original Teen Queen,* (Honesdale, Boyds Mills Press, 2010), page 80.

# BIBLIOGRAPHY

**Primary Sources**

Caesar, Julius. *The Gallic Wars*. Translated by W.A. McDevitte and W.S. Bohn. The Internet Classic Archives, 1994–2009. http://classics.mit.edu/Caesar/gallic.html.

Dio, Cassus. *Roman History*, vol. 5, Loeb Classical Library Edition, 1917, LacusCurtius, Roman Antiquity Sources. http://penelope.uchicago.edu/Thayer/e/roman/texts/cassius_dio/55.html.

Herodotus. *The Histories*. Perseus Digital Library at Tufts University. http://www.perseus.tufts.edu/hopper/text?doc=Perseus:text:1999.01.0126.

Pliny the Elder. *The Natural Histories*. Perseus Digital Library (Public domain). http://www.perseus.tufts.edu/hopper/text?doc=Perseus%3Atext%3A1999.02.0137%3Abook%3D30%3Achapter%3D4.

Polyaenus. *Stratagems of War: Book 8*. Translated by R. Shepherd, 1793. *Attalus.org*. http://www.attalus.org/translate/polyaenus8B.html.

Seutonius. *The Lives of the Twelve Caesars*. Loeb Classical Library, 1913. LacusCurtius, Roman Antiquity Sources. http://penelope.uchicago.edu/Thayer/E/Roman/Texts/Suetonius/12Caesars/Julius.html.

Strabo. *Geography*. Translated by H. L. Jones, 1917 (Public domain). LacusCurtius, Roman Antiquity Sources. http://penelope.uchicago.edu/Thayer/E/Roman/Texts/Strabo/home.html.

Tacitus. *The Annals of Imperial Rome*. Translated by J. Jackson, Loeb Classical Library, 1925–1937. LacusCurtius, Roman Antiquity Sources. http://penelope.uchicago.edu/Thayer/E/Roman/Texts/Tacitus/Annals/14B.html.

Vopiscus, Flavian. "The Life of Aurelian." *Historia Augusta*. Translated by D. Magie. Loeb Classical Library, 1921. LacusCurtius, Roman Antiquity Sources. http://penelope.uchicago.edu/Thayer/E/Roman/Texts/Historia_Augusta/home.html.

## Secondary Sources

Alvear Shecter, Vicky. *Alexander the Great Rocks the World*. Plain City: Darby Creek Publishing, 2006.

Alvear Shecter, Vicky. *Cleopatra Rules! The Amazing Life of the Original Teen Queen*. Honesdale: Boyds Mills Press, 2010.

Armelagos, G. et al. *Tetracyclines in Biology, Chemistry and Medicine*, eds, M. Nelson, W. Hillen, R.A. Greenwald. Basel, Switzerland: Springer Basel AG, 2001.

Beck, Roger, et al. *Understanding World Societies: Volume 1: to 1600*. New York: Bedford/St. Martin's, 2012.

Bianchi, Robert. *Daily Life of the Nubians*. Westport: Greenwood Press, 2004.

Bich, Nguyen and Nghia Vo. *The Trung Sisters Revisited*. Lexington: CreateSpace, 2015.

Burnstein, Stanley, editor. *Ancient Africa Civilizations: Kush and Axum*. Princeton: Markus Weiner Publishers, 2010.

Cooney, Kara. *The Woman Who Would Be King: Hatshepsut's Rise to Power in Ancient Egypt*. New York: Crown, 2014.

Curtis, Vesta S. and Sarah Stewart. *Birth of the Persian Empire: The Idea of Iran, Volume I*. London: I.B. Tauris, 2005.

Dreyfus, Renée, Keller, Cathleen, and Roehrig, Catharine (eds). *Hatshepsut: From Queen to Pharaoh*. New Haven, CT: Yale University Press, 2005.

Exhibition, Rita J. and Stanley H. Kaplan Family Foundation Gallery, *Gold and the Gods: Jewels of Ancient Nubia*, Boston Museum of Fine Arts, Boston. https://www.mfa.org/exhibitions/gold-and-gods.

Eluère, Christane. *The Celts: Conquerors of Ancient Europe*. New York: Harry N. Abrams, 1993.

Falola, Toyin. *Key Events in African History: A Reference Guide*. Westport, CT: Greenwood Press, 2002.

Fisher, Marjorie, et al. *Ancient Nubia: African Kingdoms on the Nile*. Cairo: American University in Cairo Press, 2012.

147

Fraser, Antonia. *The Warrior Queens: The Legends and Lives of the Women Who Have Led Their Nations in War*. New York: Anchor Books, 1990.

Freeman, Philip. *The Philosopher and the Druids: A Journey Among the Ancient Celts*. New York: Simon & Schuster, 2006.

Garms, David. *With the Dragon's Children*. Victoria, BC: Friesen Press, 2015.

Goldsworthy, Adrian. *Augustus: First Emperor of Rome*. New Haven: Yale University Press, 2014.

Gritzner, Charles and Douglas Phillips. *Vietnam*. New York: Chelsea House Publishers, 2006.

Group, David W. *Encyclopedia of Mind Enhancing Foods, Drugs and Nutritional Substances*. Jefferson, NC: McFarland and Company, Inc., Publishers, second revised edition, 2015.

Hale, John R. *Lords of the Sea: The Epic Story of the Athenian Navy and the Birth of Democracy*. New York: Viking, 2009.

Harkless, Necia D. *Nubian Pharaohs and Meroitic Kings: The Kingdom of Kush*. Bloomington: AuthorHouse, 2006.

Matyszak, Philip. *The Enemies of Rome: From Hannibal to Attila the Hun*. New York: Thames and Hudson, 2009.

Mayor, Adrienne. *The Amazons: Lives and Legends of Warrior Women across the Ancient World*. Princeton: Princeton University Press, 2014.

McKay, John P. et al., *Understanding World Societies, Volume I, 2nd Ed.* Boston, MA: Bedford, St. Martins, 2015.

Monderson, Frederick. *Hatshepsut's Temple at Deir el Bahari*. Bloomington: AuthorHouse, 2007.

Morkot, Robert. *The Black Pharaohs: Egypt's Nubian Rulers*. London: Rubicon Press, 2000.

Phillips, Douglas A. *Vietnam*. New York: Chelsea House, 2006.

Rilly, Claude and Alex de Voogt. *The Meroitic Language and Writing System*. Cambridge: Cambridge University Press, 2012.

Robins, Gay. *Reflections of Women in the New Kingdom: Ancient Egyptian Art from the British Museum*. San Antonio: Van Siclen Books, 1995.

Robins, Gay. *Women in Ancient Egypt*. Cambridge: Harvard University Press, 1993.

Sandler, Stanley. *Ground Warfare: An International Encyclopedia, Volume 1*. Santa Barbara, CA: ABC-CLIO, 2002.

Service, Pamela. *The Ancient African Kingdom of Kush*. Tarrytown: Benchmark Books, 1998.

Southern, Pat. *Empress Zenobia: Palmyra's Rebel Queen*. London: Continuum, 2008.

Spalinger, Anthony J. *War in Ancient Egypt: The New Kingdom*. Hoboken: John Wiley & Sons, 2008.

Stoneman, Richard. *Palmyra and Its Empire: Zenobia's Revolt against Rome*. Ann Arbor: The University of Michigan Press, 1994.

Strauss, Barry. *The Battle of Salamis: The Naval Encounter That Saved Greece—and Western Civilization*. New York: Simon and Schuster, 2004.

Taylor, Keith Weller. *The Birth of Vietnam*. Berkeley: University of California Press, 1991.

Trow, M. J. *Boudicca: The Warrior Queen*. Gloucestershire: Sutton Publishing, 2003.

Tyldesley, Joyce. *Hatshepsut: The Female Pharaoh*. London: Penguin Books, 1996.

Watson, Alaric. *Aurelian and the Third Century*. London: Routledge, 1999.

Webster, Graham. *Boudica: The British Revolt against Rome AD 60*. London: Routledge, 1978.

Woodruff, Paul. *First Democracy: The Challenge of an Ancient Idea*. New York: Oxford University Press, 2005.

## Articles

Burke, Jason. "Dig Uncovers Boudicca's Brutal Streak." *Guardian Unlimited*, 3 Dec. 2000.

Carney, Elizabeth D. "Women and Military Leaders in Pharaonic Egypt." *Greek, Roman, and Byzantine Studies*, no. 42, 2001.

Chonchirdsin, Sud. "Why a Proverb Calls the Vietnamese the 'Children of the Dragon and the Grandchildren of the Fairy.'" Scroll.in.com, March 8, 2017, https://scroll.in/article/830807/why-the-vietnamese-are-called-the-children-of-the-dragon-and-grandchildren-of-the-fairy.

Gilbert, Marc Jason. "When Heroism is Not Enough: Three Women Warriors of Vietnam, Their Historians and World History." *World History Connected*, Hawaii Pacific University, June 2007. http://worldhistoryconnected.press.illinois.edu/4.3/gilbert.html.

Hawass, Zahi. "The Scientific Search for Hatshepsut's Mummy." *KMT: A Modern Journal of Ancient Egypt*, vol. 18, no. 3, Fall 2007.

Issa, Philip. "Syrian Army Re-enters Town of Palmyra as IS Defenses Crumble." *Associated Press*, 2 Mar. 2017.

Jones, Prudence. "Rewriting Power: Zenobia, Aurelian, and the *Historia Augusta*." *Classical World*, vol. 109, no. 2, Johns Hopkins University Press, Winter 2016, pp. 221–233.

Lendering, Jona. "Earth and Water." *Livius: Articles on Ancient History*, 1997. http://www.livius.org/articles/concept/earth-and-water.

Long, Jacqueline. "Vaballathus and Zenobia (270–272 AD)." *Roman-Emperors.org*, Loyola University of Chicago, 28 July 1997.

Romey, Kristin. "City of Victory." *ARCHAEOLOGY*, vol. 55, no. 4, July/August 2002.

Smith, Roff. "London's Big Dig Reveals Amazing Layers of History." *National Geographic*, February 2016. http://ngm.nationalgeographic.com/2016/02/artifacts-found-under-london-archaeology-text.

Tyldesley, Joyce. "Hatshepsut and Tuthmosis: A Royal Feud?" *BBC History*, Oct. 2001.

Wade, Nicholas. "A United Kingdom? Maybe." *New York Times*,
6 March 2007.

Weingarten, Judith. "Hatshepsut and the Tomb Beneath the Tomb."
*Zenobia: Empress of the East*, 15 Mar. 2009. http://judithweingarten.
blogspot.com/2009/03/hatshepsut-and-tomb-beneath-tomb.html.

Weingarten, Judith. "Now All Shame is Exhausted . . ." *Zenobia:
Empress of the East*, 1 June 2008. http://judithweingarten.blogspot.
com/2008/06/now-all-shame-is-exhausted.html.

Weingarten, Judith. "Why Did She Do It?" *Zenobia: Empress of the East*,
6 Jan. 2007. http://judithweingarten.blogspot.com/2007/01/why-did-
she-do-it.html.

Williamson, Mitch. "Zenobia and Aurelian's March to Syria," *Weapons
and Warfare: History and Hardware of Warfare.* July 13, 2017.
https://weaponsandwarfare.com/2017/07/13/zenobia-and-aureli-
ans-march-to-syria/.

Wilson, Elizabeth. "The Queen Who Would be King." *Smithsonian*, Sep.
2006.

Workman, Karen. "When You're Named Isis for the Goddess, Not the
Terror Group." *New York Times*, 20 Nov. 2015.

"World Heritage Committee inscribes five new sites in Colombia, Sudan,
Jordan, Italy and Germany," UNESCO.com, June 25, 2011, http://
whc.unesco.org/en/news/771/.

Young, Gayle. "A Worthy Warrior Queen: Perceptions of Zenobia in
Ancient Rome." MA thesis, Georgetown University, June 2009.

# INDEX

Page numbers in **boldface** refer to
images and/or captions

**A**

Ahura Mazda (Persian god), 48
Amazons, 52–53, 57, 129, 133,
    136
Amanirenas, queen, **9**, 60–77, **60**,
    **62–63, 74, 75**
    battles with Rome, 65–67
    loss of eye in battle, 65
Amun,
    Egyptian Creator God, 16,
        19–20, 27
    Hatshepsut's claim as daughter,
        19–20
    in Nubia, 72
Antibiotic, ancient use of, 73–74
Apedemak, Nubian god, 71–72
Artemisia, **9**, 32–59, **32, 34–35,
    55, 58**
    invasion of Latmus, 33
    maneuvers at sea, 43–46
    war strategy, 40–44
    Xerxes, with, 37–45, 47, **58**

**B**

Boudicca, **9**, 94–117, **94, 96–97,
    115, 117**
    attacks, 101–107
    chariot, **94**, 103
    speech, 106

**C**

Caesar(s),
    Aurelian, 124–129, 131
    Augustus, 66, 67–68, 136
    Claudius, 98
    Julius, 95, 98, 109, 115, 116
Celts, 95, 98–116
    Iceni, 95
Chariots,
    Boudicca, 103
    Egypt, 18
Chinese,
    General, Wave-Calming, 84
    Han Dynasty, 78
    strongholds, 82
    taxes, 79
Confucianism, 88–89

**D**

Deir el-Bahri, 17, **28**
    Democracy, 54–55
Dragon, Vietnamese Legend of,
    88, **93**
Druids/Druidism, 100–101,
    110–112

**E**

Empire,
    Chinese, 78–90
    Egyptian, 11–27
    Nubian, 60–74
    Persian, 32–55, 118, 126–127
    Roman, 94–114, 118–133
Eye, loss of, Amanirenas, 65

**F**

Fairy, Vietnamese Legend of, 88

**G**

Greeks, 32–55

152

Athens, 37, 38, 41
    gods, 48–52
    ships, 43–47
    Sparta, 37–38

**H**

Han Dynasty, 78
Hatshepsut, 9, 11–31, 11, **12–13**, **28, 30, 64**

**I**

Iceni, Celtic tribe, 95
Invasion,
    Brittania (ancient Britain),
      94–108
    Egypt, 11–24
    Greece, 32–47
    Nubia, 61–69
    Palmyra, 118–130
    Vietnam, 78–90

**J**

Julius Caesar, 61, 95, 98, 109, 116

**K**

Kush, 27, 61
    Amanirenas, 60
    arts, 70, **76**
    Hatshepsut, 64

**L**

Lady Trieu, 90
Lindow Man, 113–114, **117**
London/Londinium, 103–104

**M**

Maat, 21, 24
Meroe/Meroitic, 61, 74
Mithras, Mithraism, 48

Mummy,
    Hatshepsut's, 25–26
    identification of, 26
    religious significance, 25

**N**

Naval battle (Artemisia), 43–44
Neferure (Hatshepsut's daughter), 15
Nubia
    Eighteenth Dynasty Egypt, in, 17
    Amanirenas, queen, 60–77
    antibiotic use, 73–74
    people, 61, 69–74
    pyramids, 69
    weapons, 70–71

**P**

Palmyra,
    ancient, 118–133
    modern, 132
Parthenon, 54–55
Persia,
    gods, 48
    multicultural kingdom, 36
    respect for women, 39
Pharaoh,
    divinity, 19, 27
    duties, 21, 24
    Hatshepsut, becoming, 19, 24
Pyramids,
    Egypt, 27
    Sudan, 69

**R**

Rome,
    General Aurelian (Caesar),
        124–131
    General, Paulinus, 102–108
    General, Petronius, 66–67
    General, Julius Caesar, 61, 95,
        98, 109, 116

**S**

Salamis, Battle, 40–47
Sparta,
    Leonidas, King 38
    Thermopylae, 38
    300 Spartan warriors, 38

**T**

Thutmose I (Hatshepsut's father),
    14, 17
Thutmose II (Hatshepsut's brother,
    husband), 14, 15, 24
Thutmose III (Hatshepsut's
    successor), 16, 19, 21–25
Tiger, Vietnamese Legend of, 87
Triremes, 46–47
Trung Sisters (Trung Nhi, Trung
    Trac), **9**, 78–93, **78, 80–81, 91**

**V**

Vietnam,
    ancient people, 83
    legends,
        Dragon and Fairy, 88, **93**
        Lady Trieu, 90
        Pregnant general, 86
        Trung sisters' death, 86
        Tiger hunters, 87
    treatment of women, 83
    territory, 83

**W**

Warfare/weapons,
    Celtic, 104–107, 113
    Chinese, 84–86
    Egypt, 17–18
    Greek, 46–47
    Nubian, 17, 70–71
    Persian, 33–47, 125–128
Woad, 113

**X**

Xerxes, 37–38, 40–54
    Artemisia, and, 40–46

**Z**

Zenobia, **9**, 118–136, **118,**
    **120–121, 134, 135**
    Cleopatra VII, 122–123, **127,**
        **130, 131**
    Coins, 131–132, 135
Zoroastrianism, 48
Zoroaster, 48

# PICTURE CREDITS